LAZARUS

LAZARUS

André Malraux

TRANSLATED BY TERENCE KILMARTIN

Holt, Rinehart and Winston
NEW YORK

Library of Congress Cataloging in Publication Data
Malraux, André, 1901–1976.
Lazarus.
(His The mirror of limbo)
Translation of Lazare.
1. Malraux, André, 1901–1976—Biography.
2. Authors, French—20th century—Biography.
I. Title. II. Series: Malraux, André, 1901–1976.
Le miroir des limbes. English.
PQ2625.A716Z51713   843′.9′12 [B]   76-58426
ISBN 0-03-015351-4

Originally published in French under the title, *Lazare*. This edition
first published in the United States in 1977.

Lazarus is part of the second volume of *The Mirror of Limbo*.
The first volume was published under the title *Anti-Memoirs*.
A portion of this book has previously appeared in *Antaeus*.

Designer: Madelaine Caldiero
Printed in the United States of America

1 3 5 7 9 10 8 6 4 2

In memory of Christian Fouchet

Part

I

I was struck down by a form of sleeping sickness; on several occasions my legs gave way and I fell as though in a dead faint, but without loss of consciousness; then it happened twice in the same week—the second time preceded by a convulsive dizziness. Medical examinations. Physicians and specialists would be unable to confer for twelve days. In the meantime, sclerosis of the peripheral nerves and a threat to the cerebellum—thus a threat of paralysis. What sort of paralysis?

Since I am working on what may be my last book, I have returned to an event which I described in *The Walnut Trees of Altenburg* thirty years ago, one of those unforeseeable and shattering events, which, like the Children's Crusade (a hundred thousand youngsters setting off on their own to deliver Jerusalem, and being exterminated or taken into slavery), seem like History's bouts of madness: the first German gas attack, at Bolgako on the Vistula in 1916. I do not know why the Vistula attack should form part of *The Mirror of Limbo*, but I know that it must. Few "subjects" can withstand the threat of death. This one embraces a confrontation between fraternity and death and that element in man which today is fumbling for an identity, and is certainly not the individual. The oldest and profoundest Christian dialogue is conducted between Sacrifice and Evil. That attack on the Russian front has been succeeded by Verdun, the mustard gas of Flanders, Hitler and the extermination camps. This grim procession cannot obliterate the cataclysmic day when faceless humanity assumed the guise of madness, as later before the atom bomb. If the airman had blown himself up with his bomb instead of dropping it on Hiroshima, he would not be forgotten—even after another bomb; and if I return to this, it is because I am seeking the crucial region of the soul where absolute Evil is pitted against fraternity.

We know enough about what happened that day to be able to imagine it; of what happened afterward, nothing remains. Published memories stop at the field hospital; there is little hope of new discoveries after sixty years. In Alsace at the end of 1944, the names of the survivors of Bolgako were no longer known. History obliterates even men's forgetfulness: that fulguration was dissolved instantaneously in the amorphous days of war, as the Second Regiment, moving up the line with the ambulance units, broke through the Russian front.

Nothing remains of this event. Perhaps the fulguration *had* to be blotted out in order to attain its superhuman afterglow. Otherwise it might have been extinguished in the accounts of frenzies, panics, or orgies that nations are reluctant to dwell upon. That gas attack exercises on me the same powerful and perturbing effect as the great myths and the defiant "No" of Antigone and Prometheus. Archaic peoples lived out their myths; until 1911, the Emperor of China still plowed the first furrow of the year, just as the mythical emperor plowed the first furrow on earth. I have relived the unknown myth of the Vistula, because I wrote it, in another form, in 1940 when I was a prisoner of war and in 1941 after I had escaped. I put aside the fragments of this book in which my memories, my obsessions, and my premonitions jostle one another, to take it up again. I made a study of the Bolgako attack because a certain number of the soldiers involved were from Alsace. At the time, the Germans posted Alsatians to the Russian front (whence the inner freedom of my protagonist, who is fighting for Germany without enthusiasm). In 1941 I did not know that the Alsace-Lorraine Brigade would exist one day, and that I should be linked to Alsace by ties of blood. Death, which hovers over me now, sends me back to the myth which came to me thirty years ago from the other side of life.

Shakespeare, tearing the curtain aside, makes death a triviality—in the revelations of Macbeth, Hamlet, Prospero; he reveals to us what we know. With the first use of poison gas in warfare, Satan reappears in the world; but his

Scourge cannot prevail over that resurgence of the blind life instinct in the only European forest where bisons of the Quaternary period are still alive. Do we know that many examples of man and death overwhelmed by the instinctive fraternity embedded in man—"programmed," our sneering computers might say? On that day, emerging as inexplicably as the spirit of Evil, the slavering demibeast of the depths where man was born emulated the defiant gesture of Prometheus. Cornered, perhaps, by death, I take refuge in this account of one of the most enigmatic spasms of life.

The individual has no place in it. Scarcely even Major Berger. In the dugout, he listens; during the attack, he watches. The gesticulating professor counts for scarcely more than his bulldogs. The rest speak with the ageless voice of humankind, the primeval voice of the German soldiers in the trench, of the French prisoners in the camp. In the heart of the enemy, there is also mercy.

W hen the professor's car drew up, Major Berger and the adjutant saw their military salute acknowledged by the flourish of a broad-brimmed felt hat; one hand threw back a scarf covering nose and mouth (in June!), the other tossed a half-smoked cigarette at their feet. Hands, cigarette, scarf, longish gray hair—an entire dovecote flew out of the professor's face; he resembled Bismarck in the guise of a conjurer. A large, placid youth followed him out of the car, an attaché case in one hand, a basket in the other: his son.

"Delighted to meet you, gentlemen," said the professor, "really delighted. I've always had a very special respect for intelligence officers."

He knew Major Berger as the youngish anthropologist who had been an adviser to the "Red Sultan" and assistant to Enver Pasha, now defending the Dardanelles against the Allies. Berger knew the professor as one of the few specialists in gas warfare, a man far more interested in gas than in the shabby affairs of the intelligence department that cluttered his days.

"Let's go and dine."

He linked arms with the astonished Berger. The Europa was the least dilapidated of the three requisitioned hotels in Bolgako. Beneath the calm evening sky and the vague scent of dusty roses not yet withered, a rumble of guns reverberated in the solitude of the vicarage garden.

The table was laid in Berger's room. With a mournful air the professor put his large hat on the mantelpiece, drew a flask and a yellow bottle out of his basket, and took a gulp from the mouth of the bottle.

"For my asthma, gentlemen. But this" (he held up the flask) "this, mark you, is genuine French brandy. Absolutely."

Gloomily he put it down on the table.

"Let's eat. Tomorrow morning the Russians will be crushed."

Still dejected.

Berger went down to fetch the beer. When he returned, with a bunch of beer bottles sprouting from each fist, the professor, his son, and the adjutant were bent over two photographs. The first, lying between the dinner plates, was of the professor's house. It was about to be pulled down to make room for an airfield. He had hoped to save it, but one of the telegrams awaiting him here had brought a final refusal. Hence his dismay. The other photograph was of the adjutant's two children.

"Now it's my turn to show you my children," said the professor's son.

Berger looked: three bulldogs.

"Heinz was a student at Oxford," his father said. "Then he specialized in animal medicine. By choice, mark you."

"By inclination," murmured big Heinz sleepily. And bowing slightly as though introducing himself, he added in a humbly self-satisfied tone: "Veterinary surgeon."

He looked like a bulldog, only flabbier.

"Is it merely a trial run tomorrow, professor, or a real attack? Since the first attempt failed ..."

"The tests that have been made on this front up to now, I ask you!"

He burst into childish laughter: like the great apes, this mustachioed savant was alternately senile and infantile, never young.

"They tried to use poison. But that's absolutely idiotic. Prussic acid and carbon monoxide are perfect poisons, but what results did they produce? You need half a gram of prussic acid per cubic meter of air: the victim is seized with convulsions and falls dead in a tetanic rigor. It's perfect in an enclosed space. But battlefields, you see, happen to be in the open air!

"So then what? Carbon monoxide was tried. In laboratory conditions a deadly poison, possessing all the requisite qualities, easy to prepare, and cheap. It congeals the hemoglobin in the blood, prevents it from mixing with the oxygen in the air. But there's still the problem of the open air.

"I've discarded poisons. We're going to use ... something else. We've gone beyond chlorine derivatives. Chlorine's not so bad, you know. Easy to liquefy, intolerable to the human organism, and very cheap, mark you. According to your ... colleagues on the western front, gentlemen, our chemical attack on the Yser caused between ten and twenty thousand cases of instantaneous poisoning: more than enough to break through the English line. Absolutely. But if the enemy uses masks, we'll have to begin all over again."

"When you disperse poisons," Berger asked, "what do you aim for?"

The professor spread his arms in a balletic gesture.

"The mucous membrane, major. It's quite simple: the mucous membrane. We have more effective compounds than chlorine, naturally: phosgene is ten times more virulent than chlorine, but phosgene ..."

He crossed to the open window and put out his hand to test the wind. Beyond the garden, the crosses and onion domes of an Orthodox church glowed in the evening light at the far end of the sloping square. As the professor's voice enumerated the virtues and defects of phosgene, Berger reflected on the extent of the Slavic world stretching as far as the Pacific.

The professor threw his extinguished cigarette out of the window, which he then closed, and came back beaming with pleasure:

"The wind's still excellent, still excellent. But actually I'm not so much afraid of a change of wind as of a sudden damp...."

He had already lit another cigarette and gone back to his dinner.

"But we're still at a prehistoric stage in chemical warfare. Ethyl dichloride sulfate is perhaps the ideal combat gas. A caustic product, blistering and poisonous at the same time. Particularly dangerous, mark you, because the victim is not affected at the actual moment of poisoning: it begins to take effect several hours later.... And it's effective up to one part in fourteen million parts of air!"

And, waving the photograph of his house as though by way of proof, he went on:

"There's no doubt that chemistry is the ultimate weapon, the superior weapon that will confer on those who handle it properly—who master it—worldwide supremacy.... Absolutely. Perhaps the mastery of the world, do you realize!"

"Is the enemy's intelligence service likely to get hold of our formulas?" asked the adjutant.

"In less than six months we shall have used six different gases. Mark you, the race between the use of gas and the means of protection against it is going to be the same that started thousands of years ago, ever since the bludgeon was first invented—between the lance and the breastplate, the bullet and armor-plating. But ... and this is the all-important point ..."

The photograph slipped from his hand. He stooped to pick it up without breaking off:

"...ever since that struggle began, protective armor has never won the last round."

"You did say, professor, did you not, that the new discoveries make it possible to poison the enemy troops without their knowing it?"

Once again the professor brandished the photograph of his house:

"One part in fourteen million parts of air! If you look at it from an objective point of view, gas constitutes the most humane method of warfare. Absolutely. Because gas announces its presence. The sclera first of all goes blue, the breath begins to hiss, the iris—it's fascinating to note—turns almost black. In short, the enemy is forewarned. Now, if I feel I have a chance, however infinitesimal, I'm brave; but if I know I haven't, courage ... phooey!"

"It will be a great misfortune," said the adjutant, "if we're to see the old German tradition of warfare vanish from the empire."

"Yes," replied the professor dryly. "But Germans are men too, and capable of weakness, are they not? Sulfate is incorruptible."

An hour later, the professor was aware that the young anthropologist was interested only in mankind, the adjutant only in Germans; and Berger realized that the professor was interested only in gas warfare, and Heinz only in dogs. The professor had known before he arrived that Berger's friends had nicknamed him "Frigate," and this name of a bird or a ship was not inappropriate to his prowlike face. Inwardly Berger thought of the professor alternately as "Bulldog" or "Bismarck." The wind had not changed; the cannonade had ceased; a sound of shovels could be heard in the distance, above the sad, slow clip-clop of a horse's hooves. A troop of cavalry was gliding by in the depths of the night; there was too much war at ground level for metaphysical anguish. The cool night breeze was blowing gently and steadily toward Russia.

At six o'clock in the morning, Berger was waiting for the professor and the adjutant in the covered trench which communicated with the front-line trenches. The order for the attack was not to be given before their arrival. Berger had been installed in a small dugout (reserved for the command?) off the main trench, a vast cellar from whose observation slits diagonal bars of daylight flashed like swords raised in salute. He only saw the soldiers when they crossed these mote-filled beams. Nearly all of them were sitting on the ground, talking.

"The tsar!" said the loudest voice. "Annihilate Germany!" (Someone folded up a newspaper.) "Annihilate Germany! He stays in his palace, in Petersburg. Underground. It's pathetic. And people are twats enough to listen to him! One thing you can say for Frederick the Great: at least he put himself at the head of his army and marched out in front."

General hubbub.

"The French haven't any rifles left," said another voice parenthetically.

"You're the sort of clot who thinks it's a snap roll call when someone wakes you up at night to stand you a beer. And then you talk about Frederick the Great. It makes me sick!"

The argument shot off like a ferret into another shadowy corner, and was succeeded by an exchange of confidences:

"Now, my job isn't just manual, it's more brain-work. . . ."

"Are you a fitter?"

"Metal cutter."

"Yes, like me, when you're cutting you need concentration, you know, it's brain work."

The modest tone did not suggest sarcasm.

A pause. Another voice continued another confidential exchange:

"The women work on the sorting. Before it was down in the pit, but now it's at the surface—there's a conveyor belt. But when you're married you can't work in the mine anymore."

"Miners aren't allowed to be married?"

"Not the men, the women. A married woman isn't allowed through the gates. That's over."

Silence once more. In the distance, the deep rumble of the guns and the bursting of shells.

"And you know, in the shafts, the galleries, you always work stripped—just trousers. And you don't have to bother about eye makeup! But coal dust's quite good for the skin.... You're lost without your lamp, though: it's your guardian angel."

In spite of the shafts of light from the observation slits, the magic respect with which the word *lamp* had been uttered was in keeping with darkness.

"There's an inspection every week—talk about a checkup! I had a little doll, a real good-looker, she was; used to polish my lamp for me every day."

A man who was reminded of love when he thought of a miner's lamp and a naked torso covered in coal dust....

Another voice, closer:

"The fellow specially asked for the captain's report to get his home leave. Been on the western front, landed up here, hadn't had a single day off. He had a five-year-old kid. At five, kids start understanding things.... Anyway—he gets his leave, arrives home, and the kid says: 'Where're you going to sleep?' 'Why, in my bed, of course,' says he. 'Oh,' says the kid, 'so the Swiss won't be coming back?' Damn me if there wasn't a Swiss sleeping with his old woman every night!"

"And then?"

"Well, nothing. He didn't exactly split his sides. But he didn't do anything about it, because of the kid."

The fury of the bombardment filled the trench.

"I know one who arrived home on leave without letting his wife know. He got there at night, and knocked. No one opened. And he knew damn well his wife was there. He went on knocking half the night. She didn't open. She didn't want to. Then he got it. He went back to his unit and hung himself. Just like that, with his belt, above his bed. And yet it was just an ordinary bed...."

Berger had had no experience of the barrack-room. But in spite of the canvas-covered pointed helmets which crossed the beams of daylight from time to time, he was hearing the secret voice of humanity, more profound than the voice of war.

"I don't believe the *Limping Messenger*, but it did say: "When the harvest has been bad and the servants' names begin with the same letter as the master's, there will be war...."

"Hindenburg ..."

No one mentioned the name *Hohenzollern*. Berger knew the *Limping Messenger*, one of those old almanacs published in Strasbourg. "When the harvest has been bad ..." The age-old peasant link between the unpredictable harvest and man's unpredictable fate.

"Which side wins, in the prophecy? Ours?"

"No."

"What do we care? The *Messenger*'s just another bit of Alsatian bunk."

"I don't know. Of course, nobody wants anything to do with Alsatians."

"Shut your trap. There's quite a few of them here."

Farther off, someone was saying:

"By the time we got there they'd already been raped by the Cossacks and the Austrians, they hardly complained anymore...."

A number of soldiers who were not wearing shirts had unbuttoned their tunics.

"You don't know the Lutheran cross!" said a hoarse voice in answer to a question Berger had not heard. "What *do* you know?"

A different voice from those he had heard until then—plebeian still, but restrained, and with the hint of a smile. A ray of light on someone's chest brought out with electric brilliance the glittering arms of a cross and the luminous bead of the Huguenot dove. The same voice once again answered a question:

"I'm not a believer, but I like to go to church from time to time. Provided I'm on my own. In certain circumstances. . . ."

"What circumstances?"

"If I'm unhappy. . . . Or if I want to remember. . . ."

The speakers moved away. There was a fairly long pause: the guns were now firing only intermittently, and the footsteps of the men Berger had just heard—NCOs—came back toward him.

"With volunteers there's always a moral problem. Look, just now I needed three of them, and this gas business can often be . . . serious. I picked the three nicest. Why? Because that's what they wanted: they were keen and I wanted to be nice. In fact, by being nice I may have condemned them to death. And I should have chosen the ones whose death would matter least."

"And how do you solve the moral problem?"

Berger could not hear the answer: a shrug, probably. He

was surprised that the NCOs had been told of the nature of the attack. Another voice revealed that the troops were also onto it:

"When I was still working in the Ruhr, we came to a shaft where there'd been a firedamp explosion a long time ago. There was a workman with his pick in his hand just as if he was still alive, and a horse behind him which still looked as if it was pulling the skip. The gas had preserved them, but we brought in the air. We'd been there only ten minutes when both the man and the nag were dust. What you grinning at, damn fool? I tell you it's true!"

An unprecedented uproar stirred the darkness, from which eventually emerged:

"I'll tell you what gas does. . . ."

It was the slow, solemn voice of the people in the face of mystery, the voice that makes one suspect that the voices of the sorcerers of old were equally childish:

"I'll tell you about gas. The poor bastard who catches it, well, he stays stock-still. Stock-still he stays. Can't move. Just as he was when he caught it, just the same. Playing cards, for instance. . . ."

"Dead before you know it."

"And if the wind changes?"

"The command has organized the attack," an NCO shouted.

"That's what they say," someone answered weakly.

That was all, until a new gas specialist spoke up:

"They tried it out on the western front. When the Frenchies got there they were caught off guard; there was a bunch of gravediggers taking the dead to a cemetery, near the chapel of rest, and they just stuck there, their toes turned up alongside the dead in the blankets. All exactly alike, like dummies in shop windows."

"Oh, come off it. Just because you're a gravedigger you don't have to give us all that crap."

"Their toes turned up, I tell you, you stupid bastard!"

"Oh, all right, all right."

"I tell you, they just stuck there."

They did not know that there is no such thing as a chapel of rest in France. The voices rose, in accordance with the technique of popular argument, which is to repeat the same thing more and more loudly. A cannonade drowned the discussion.

"A road-sweeper stopped dead in his tracks, his broom upside down—think of it!"

"A pig being killed, knife in his belly, but now he can't squeal!"

Was it the men speaking, or their jobs?

Making a joke of it enabled them to muse aloud without embarrassment. Each of them saw life suddenly brought to a stop—not so much the enemy's as his own.

"The bookkeeper who can't finish his accounts," murmured a shy voice.

"They're not as special as they say, those things, gas and gadgets and all. Those people don't know nothing about animals. If you make a slit in a mule's muzzle, it can't bray anymore, so you don't hear it. Think what you could do with mules like that—a cavalry the other side couldn't hear."

I'm listening perhaps to those who are about to die,

Berger thought. Each one thinks he is speaking about himself. . . . But how long have the gods been hearing them? The gods of the forest, Charlemagne. . . . One speaks of the "German people." It's a creation of their own minds, a sort of costume, like the uniform they've adopted. Ancient Christendom . . . the white race, perhaps. . . .

He remembered Central Asia, the caravanserais. The steppes, the little fires, the vast sky—a similar murmur, like the voice of the earth. God much more present. But did not the inarticulate babbling he was listening to plunge deeper into time, into mankind, beyond the divine words?

"The Frenchies are calling up kids of seventeen. Half of them desert."

"There'll be a revolution; it's a country that's always having a revolution."

"Shut your traps!"

The gas interested them more than the French.

"Anyway, what are you talking about? A blacksmith stock-still with his hammer just about to strike the anvil! That's a load of balls—the hammer'd fall because it's too heavy."

"The electric light would stay on all right. . . ."

Berger thought of the city in the *Arabian Nights* where all human gestures, the life of flowers, the flames of lamps were suspended by the Angel of Death. The petrified gestures of the legendary blacksmiths under a light scarcely dimmed by the passage of human wills, ephemeral as this war and its armies. The man who had just spoken about electric light, a man with the face of a hereditary alcoholic, rummaged in a wretched little valise, a sort of doll's case. The darkness was once more peopled. The pitch of the voices varied, but the tone remained the same—the same resignation, the same spurious authority, the same absurd science and the same experience, the same inexhaustible sadness and the same inexhaustible gaiety, and the arguments that simply consisted of increasingly vehement assertions, as though these voices from the darkness were incapable of individualizing their anger.

Time there was once again military time, dependent on orders from above. Beneath one of the shafts of daylight, clearly visible on the carboniferous soil, a pack of tarot cards was spread out, and a hand would pick out a card from time to time, with a murmur that bespoke an effort to foretell a life. This disembodied hand seemed to scurry across the cards like a rodent, for all eternity.

After another silence, a voice whispered in a tone of affectionate apology:

"I didn't marry her for her looks."

Was one of the men showing someone else a photograph? His words assumed a mysterious intensity in the darkness. In the shafts of daylight no one was showing anyone anything. Under the nearest one a youth with delicate features sat reading. What was he doing in this territorial regiment? Was it he who had just spoken? He had not moved once since Berger had been listening. Crouching in the shaft of light from the observation slit, he was reading. How low the roof of the trench was!

Two figures passed by, vaguely silhouetted against a

faint nimbus of light: the photograph was illuminated by the tiny flame of a lighter. With the same resignation, the hoarse voice that had said "I go to church when I want to remember" replied:

"Oh well, you know, my wife isn't much to look at either."

The gravedigger came back.

"... But you see, they found a dog. It was all right for us to keep it, wasn't it? 'Cause we hadn't paid for it. My wife called it Peterl, almost the same name as me. My little girl had never been able to pronounce her father's name. Well, believe it or not, ever since we've had the dog she says 'Peter' just like everyone else!"

The voice became bitter:

"She couldn't manage it for me. But still, I suppose it's something."

The shafts of daylight dimmed: a flight of migrant birds was sweeping across the sky toward the Vistula. Through the thick penumbra Berger listened to the voice of the only species that knows—however dimly—that it can die.

Suddenly all the men in the trench rose. Someone had just come in:

"Gas masks on! The Hundred and Thirty-second first!"

Berger realized why the soldiers knew that they were going to follow the gas attack.

They collected their equipment, in the darkness streaked with daylight, and headed toward the sap with a clanking of mess kits, rifles, and buckles, on their way to the front line. Their captain came to fetch Berger, and they were the last to leave. The playing cards had been left on the ground, as had the book which the young man with the face of a student had been reading: *The Adventures of Three Scouts*. Would the soldiers be coming back, then? They were moving off in single file, only their backs visible. Having reached the sap, they appeared in profile, the snouts of their gas masks jutting out in front of them. Through a slit cut obliquely into the parapet, Berger glimpsed the no-man's-land which separated them from the Russian trenches, bright after the darkness of the dugout. Against the green background already yellowing in the summer sun, great waves of umbelliferous flowers swayed in the wind. The German first-line trenches were a little farther away, above a frieze of half-withered flowers which the wind formed into an elaborate tracery in the distance and shook furiously in front of the observation slits. Two facing slopes, and the river at the bottom. The Russian slope rose so peacefully that the barbed wire entanglements seemed like fences on pastureland. Not a man, not an animal in sight. The guns had stopped firing. It was a prewar summer scene.

An elongated dust cloud rose in the sunlight. Not in a plume, as in the wake of an automobile, but uniform in height and thickness, like a wall. It kept on growing, although no engine could be heard. The road disappeared; the emission of the gas had begun.

Once by one, four ambulances drew up beside some copses in front of the trenches.

There was a rush for the observation slits. With his arms folded, the professor stood beneath one, a Bismarckian daddy longlegs fingering his scarf, with which he sought to muffle up his moustaches. The sheet of gas had reached the parallel trunks of an apple orchard, then their branches. The bottom of the valley was now just a yellow fog, reddening alongside the fields and the young fir trees, from which protruded the ghostly shape of a tall telegraph pole.

Spreading out like a sheet, with a width of half a mile, the gas rolled toward the Russian advanced positions. It curled into a wood, shrouded the bases of the fir trees while leaving their tops visible, and reappeared farther on, so that the sawtooth crests stood out against a background of fog as in a Japanese print. It continued its sluggish ascent, covering the plowed fields that rose in strips toward the high ground, the meadows purple with clover, the last of the rye, and the huge rectangles dotted with hayricks, and finally, at the highest point, near the Russian trenches, the copses growing thicker and thicker, and the ragged stretch of forest hacked into clearings by the pounding of the artillery. Nothing moved there.

Then something came dashing out from the Russian lines toward the advancing gas: a horse, which appeared minute even through binoculars. The gas seemed to be moving much faster now that it was approaching the trenches. The horse dashed toward it, riderless, with the rhythmic movement of galloping seen from a distance. It stopped, spun round, then set off again toward the left, and the clatter of hooves on a road carried across the ground, astonishingly clear, much closer than that tiny galloping horse in the immensity of the landscape. A whinny came echoing across the valley. Through the binoculars, the horse could be seen raising its head in the air like a dog howling. It galloped off again, heading straight into the gas. Its hooves could no longer be heard. It was swallowed up in the silence.

It did not reappear; the endless, silent advance of the gas, which seemed destined to continue to the ends of the earth, the dying whinny, the almost clean-cut edges of the pall began to give this fog the menacing aspect of a war machine.

Had the Russians abandoned their positions? It was difficult, even with the binoculars, to gauge the moment when the gas would reach their trenches. Soon they would be submerged; and, apart from this horse, like a creature from the Apocalypse, whinnying in the sunlight before plunging headlong as though in self-immolation, nothing had emerged from them. It was impossible for them to have been evacuated. At the bottom of the valley, the small clump of fir trees and the telegraph pole and its insulators had disappeared under the accumulating gas; halfway up, a few treetops still protruded. The tufts of grass and the slender thistles concealing the observation slit were now silhouetted against the russet-tinged milky background of the gas. The professor, his nose twitching between the eyepieces of his binoculars, was leaning on Berger with all his weight.

Had the enemy found a means of stopping the gas, which seemed to hang motionless at the edge of the parapet? The wind swept a new wave of it forward, and this wave continued to advance as though it were overtaking the first. Berger remembered what the professor had said:

"The sclera first of all goes blue, the breath starts to hiss, the iris—it's really most odd—turns almost black. . . . None of the Russians will be able to bear the pain."

Was this what was happening beneath that fog in which nothing moved, and which was still advancing with the writhing movements of a prehistoric reptile, as though it would never stop until it reached the end of the earth?

"When our troops get there, will there be no more gas left in the trenches?"

"There's nothing to worry about," the professor answered sharply; "the gas will be cleared, and there's always the field hospital. It's not a question of staying there! And besides, I . . ."

His sentence was cut short by a frenzied renewal of the Russian guns. They pounded the gas as they might have pounded an enemy onslaught. The shells burst spasmodically, red flashes in the dense pall which had now turned yellow again; when they lacerated its edges, the shreds moved forward a little faster than the mass itself, without, however, detaching themselves completely. Flickering with its red gleams like a river in the beams of the setting sun, the gas continued its imperturbable advance like an inexorable scourge, revealed as what it was: a deadly weapon.

As suddenly as it had broken out, the Russian artillery stopped firing.

"Anyone who feels symptoms of poisoning," a commanding voice immediately shouted in the trench, "remember now: immediate withdrawal to the field hospital. A taste of bitter almonds, breath hissing . . . Is that clear?"

When Berger and his companions left the trench, the gas had disappeared over the far side of the ridge; all that remained of it was the Japanese mist at the bottom of the valley, and a blackish trail over everything it had touched, as though it had left in its wake a stretch of winter under the radiant sky. Still no sign of life from the Russian trenches.

A few companies of infantry, which had set off much earlier, were crossing the river. Berger could see them clearly. Could the Russians see them too? Through the vast, stagnant banks of mist men were creeping forward as if through a swamp, separating, joining up again. Around the tops of the fir trees, wisps of russet cloud were blown about by the wind. Once the river was behind them, the companies took up battle formation without halting their advance.

Everyone was on tenterhooks for the first shell that would herald the renewal of the Russian artillery barrage—massacre, pulverization.

Through his binoculars Berger picked up his 132nd, which was now among the advance companies. Under the rows of canvas-covered spiked helmets, like Saracens' helms, the tiny bodies concealed the barbed wire barrier; the jolting advance came to a halt, and the human blobs began to get entangled in the network of wires, to kick about in it like flies in a spider's web. The stubborn advance, slowed down by distance as the gas had been, gave way to a static puppet show. Then they all disappeared into the Russian trench, or beyond.

No, some of them remained on the barbed wire. Fresh companies arrived, wavered, plunged. The whole brigade advanced. Only the wind could be heard, and not a man could now be seen on the entire battlefield. No sign of war, only the dazzling sun on the broad rustic landscape, on the wooden town still strangely intact over there with its onion-shaped domes. But neither Berger nor the adjutant took their eyes off the almost imperceptible line of the Russian trenches.

The professor's binoculars, which seemed to be jammed into his eye sockets, were shaking. The infantry had been ordered to push on toward the second enemy lines, and to occupy as quickly as possible the copses behind the ridge that was now concealed by the advancing gas; yet not one of the soldiers had reappeared.

"Could they have been gassed themselves?" Berger asked at last.

The professor shrugged his shoulders furiously, and his quivering binoculars went out of focus.

"They were told not to stay there! They were ordered not to stay there! Of course, if they spend their lives there...."

His left hand let go of the shaking binoculars and clutched Berger's arm. A man in shirt-sleeves had just emerged from the Russian trench.

A man seven feet tall, with tiny legs. Without a gas mask. He stopped, fell down. From one end of the trench to the other men in shirt-sleeves, white blobs clearly visible in spite of the distance, emerged without masks. All of them too tall, like fairground giants with heads bobbing up and down on the end of invisible broomsticks. Why the devil had the soldiers taken off their tunics and gas masks?

A number of fairground giants came apart. The shirt-sleeved half of the body fell off, while the other half walked on. They were made up of two men, one carrying the other. Were there already so many casualties? Still this silence in the wind.

The green-clad soldiers lifted the white blobs onto their shoulders again, and the hobbling procession surged through openings clipped in the barbed wire. It was not setting off toward the Russian lines; it was coming back.

Along the whole line, the troops were flooding back through the openings made by wire cutters—a confused swarm around the masked soldiers carrying the white blobs with a stumbling gait, like ants carrying their eggs. They were evacuating the Russian position. In this silence without a shell burst or a rifle shot.

The professor dropped his binoculars, which were slung round his neck on a cord, and ran forward, his muffler flying.

On Berger's left was a horse. He mounted it and galloped off. The retreating units, now more and more scattered, appeared, disappeared and reappeared, getting closer and closer. At length Berger crossed the path of two soldiers, who looked at him without seeing him. They saw nothing. They were running. They still wore their gas masks. Deep-sea divers from some distant ocean, beasts from another planet.

"What are the Russians doing?"

He yelled, but they did not hear him: the only human faculty they still retained was the ability to run. They disappeared under the trees. His horse whinnied, like the one that had plunged into the pall of gas. A soldier of the 132nd appeared. He too was running, masked but without a helmet. Berger pulled up his horse across his path:

"What's happened to the Russians?" he yelled once more.

The man answered frenziedly, with much waving of his arms and jerking of his neck. Berger motioned him to remove his gas mask. The man went on shouting. Berger made out the words *We can't!*

"What can't you do? And where are your weapons?"

"We can't! We..."

He screamed no with his hands, his shoulders, his head. He was choking. With both arms outstretched in the gesture of an orator addressing an audience, he pointed to the flesh-pink clover with its tightly clustered flowers which surrounded them, as though he were denouncing that rosy fleece between the dark walls of the trees. Then he rushed frantically away. Berger put his horse into a gallop once more. At the edge of the road, as though struck by lightning, the animal skidded, stiff-legged, for five yards, and pitched him off into the bushes. When Berger looked up again, the horse was still in the rigid, terrifying pose of a statue. Life ebbed back into the horse's lips, which parted to lay bare its teeth, then suddenly surged through its body from ears to spine; it bolted away. Berger was on the threshold of the area traversed by the gas.

He rubbed his kneecap, staring ahead; his fingers encountered something repulsive, like a tuft of dead hair, spiders' webs, floccules of accumulated dust. His boot had scraped along the ground for about a yard, filling the gap between leather and knee with clover and the flowers of wild carrot that grew among the bushes, black and viscous as though churned up from the depths of some slimy pond. The shape of the flowers was intact. So was the shape of a corpse, come to that: his hand drew back with the disgust that life feels for carrion. In the open meadow before him, over a distance of three hundred yards, the gas had left not a square inch of life. On the tufts of tall grass that now lay flattened, the sun glistened with the dull lugubrious glow it sheds on coal. A few rows of decomposed apple trees looked like lichened stumps with their dung-colored leaves plastered against the lifeless branches. Apple trees pruned by man, killed like men: more dead than the other trees, because fruitful. Beneath them, all the grass was black. Black, too, and slimy, the trees enclosing the horizon; dead the woods across which flitted a few silhouettes of German soldiers, plunging deeper into them on seeing Berger get up. Dead the leaves, dead the grass, dead the earth on which the galloping hooves of the bolting horse vanished in the wind. Berger put on his gas mask.

All that remained standing among the apple trees were

clumps of thistle, of which the heads, prickles, and leaves had all acquired the rusty hue of flowers about to crumble into dust, while their stems had taken on the repulsive whiteness of anatomical specimens in jars. The slimy meadow lay between two walls of forest. Although injured in the knee, Berger was able to walk, trailing behind him clods of earth that grew heavier and heavier. The sound of his horse's hooves had died away in the wind. Another horse, with its legs bunched up as in racing photographs, lay collapsed in front of him, perhaps the one that had charged into the pall of gas: not yet stiff, gray eyes wide open, coat rotted like the grass and the leaves, muscles contracted. Around him rose the spikes of Aaron's rod, rust-red like the thistles, but all their flowers shriveled; a swarm of dead bees clung to one of the stems, like grains on a corncob. Beyond this gateway to the valley of death, beyond the distant line of telegraph poles and wires, a few high clouds scudded across the birdless sky.

Berger moved forward heavily. Isolated in this wilderness, as though keeping vigil over the gassed horse, stood a dead tree; not rotted by the gas, but with all its branches clear-cut, angular, ossified, in the tragic posture of every dead tree on earth. This tree, petrified long since, seemed, in that universal putrefaction, to be the last remnant of life. A magpie flitted slowly by, white feathers standing out in its black wings; then dropped like a bundle of rags.

Having crossed the clearing, Berger reached the far side of the wood. It was no longer a question of walking through putrescence, but of plunging into it. The thickets of bramble and double hawthorn were lifeless, deliquescent, viscous, with the livid reddish color of dead animals that turns to black at twenty yards. The brambles no longer clung. With the disquieting sensation of having recovered his strength, Berger pushed through the thorny barrier, meeting no resistance as it melted away before his knees, his shoulders, his stomach. Only the long thorns of the acacias, whose branches did not snap at the first touch, still pricked, but their leaves hung down like boiled lettuce, with here and there a dead spider in the middle of its web beaded with greenish dew. Matted ivy hung down from the suppurating tree trunks. Each step stirred a bittersweet smell from the crushed undergrowth—the smell of the gas?

Suddenly four soldiers in gas masks appeared, covered in foliage, some of it sticking to their uniforms, some of it, less affected by the gas, blown about by the high wind like dead leaves. Without looking at each other, the soldiers advanced in single file, alone in this putrefied forest; it was scarcely possible to walk two abreast along the path. Berger barred their way, but his authority had disappeared, and he was no longer on horseback. They were as horrified as he was by these leaves, these purulent tree trunks, decomposing while still upright. The first soldier stopped less than a yard away, and lifted his gas mask.

"It's nothing to do with me," he said between clenched teeth, looking at everything except Berger with a hunted look; "nothing to do with me!"

And he took off through the trees, floundering in the slime. The second and the third came by shoulder to shoulder, as though supporting each other against Berger. One of them shouted in his face "No, no, my friend, no!" as though fed up with a long speech (perhaps the speech he had had to put up with from every one of his officers since the beginning of the war). The other was laughing hysterically, though Berger was aware of his laughter only by the ceaseless shaking of his gas mask.

Are there any casualties? Berger was thinking. The soldier went by. Berger had not voiced his thought. Not even lifted his gas mask. The last soldier, having drawn abreast of him, shook his mask, hesitated, stamped his foot, causing a shower of leaves to fall from his greatcoat, then raised his mask:

"Because I've got something to tell you, major!"

Whereupon, amazed to hear his voice filling the silence, he plunged like the others into the matted undergrowth.

Beyond the curtain of trees—the tops of some of the taller ones still green in the wind above these infernal woods—the steep slope revealed to Berger the debacle of the German infantry, with hundreds of men in shirt-sleeves being carried by others. Limping along at the double, taking shortcuts, he plunged once more through the blighted trees. The soldiers he met in their flight, plastered with leaves, did not answer his shouted questions. One of them, passing close by, glanced furtively behind him with a nervous jerk of the head. He was running away, but not from fear.

Above the deep gullies, the sordid world of the liquefied forest was silhouetted against the light. Suddenly a body emerged, pushed upward from below, again in shirt-sleeves, arms dangling as in a Descent from the Cross. Then came the man who was carrying it. The first German gas victim. Berger ran forward, fell again, ran on; the pain in his knee had become deadened.

It was not a German; it was a Russian.

But the man carrying him was a German. He lifted his gas mask and stared at Berger with a look of hatred.

"What's happened? What? What?" The German had an age-old peasant face. His deepening frown made his forehead look even lower. He gave Berger a sidelong glance. He carried the Russian on his shoulders, having thrown away his rifle. Berger thought he had shouted, and realized for the second time that he had not uttered a word. He raised his gas mask.

"An ambulance," the man said at last, menacingly, through clenched teeth.

"What's happened, for God's sake?"

Berger had recovered his voice.

"Somewhere they've got first-aid stuff!"

The man's frown deepened. He seemed much older than Berger, who felt, just as if the soldier had shouted it out, how much the man despised him for his obvious youth. The soldier gave a heave of his torso, taking care not to drop the body, brutal enough to suggest that he wanted to push the Russian's face into Berger's. The thrust of his shoulder threw the dangling head back, twisting it round to reveal, instead of the tobacco-colored hair, a hideous gas-infected face. From his greatcoat the same bittersweet odor rose as from the crushed branches. The whole movement, the way the German held the body, expressed a clumsy, heartrending brotherhood.

"Must do something," he said, a little less threateningly.

The Russian's lips and eyes were purple in his gray flesh. His nails scraped his shirt, trying to tear it off but unable to grasp it. Beneath the evil trees from which slimy leaves continued to fall, the light across the dell dappled the surrounding forest, livid with decomposition. Nearby, the wind wrinkled the stagnant water of a pond bordered with little clumps of still-intact watercress-like vegetation, in which rolled the swollen corpse of a squirrel, its tail limp. The soldier staggered off with his burden.

Berger had to get out of this incomprehensible wood in which nothing human existed or could exist. Against the sunlit void of the ravine round which he now stumbled, the tattered foliage of the lower branches, the matted leaves falling like hanging capes, the tentacles clinging to the tree trunks, all that dank paludal world stood out with the sharpness of silhouettes on a shadow-theater screen. Not only the void of the ravine, but the nearness of the forest's edge now thronged with trunks enveloped by dead algae in a powdery mist, a mist full of the sparkle of June in the falling wind, which restored the submerged forest to the peace of summer woodlands. Berger had looked at the gassed Russian's face for no more than a few seconds. In the past year he had seen his share of wounded and killed, the stiffness of the first corpses under their blankets, the ashen faces among the barbed wire entanglements; but no dead man's face would ever make him forget those terrible features.

What he was coming to was not a clearing, but another patch of open meadowland walled in by the slimy trees. The rotted grass disclosed countless little spiders' webs, intact, beaded with a poisonous dew and glistening in the harsh light from one end of the field to the other like a carpet of repulsive flowers. Amid all this nauseous shimmer a pinpoint of light stood out, glinting like a window caught by a ray of the setting sun in the evening haze. It flickered on the chest of a soldier bent under the weight of a Russian flung over his shoulders, arms on one side, legs on the other: a trinket dangled in the triangle of his shirt open to the waist. The man was now close enough for Berger to discern the dove and the crucifix, the double bead of the Huguenot cross. The sight of the little cross was like the face of a friend.

But the shaggy figure, helmetless, with windblown hair flapping over his nose, bore little resemblance to the man glimpsed in the sap. The soldier stopped, his gas mask up, the snout like a conical hat, eyelids fluttering, and straightened his back slowly, so as not to drop the body, but enough to get rid of a painful cramp.

"It's a long way," he said.

His manner seemed hostile; but as he cautiously straightened his back under the Russian's weight, his face broke into a wan smile at the desolation that surrounded them. Berger noticed his rank.

"You're an NCO? What's happ ... Why? ..."

The man shook his head and winced, for his neck was wedged under the body he was carrying. The wince did not, however, quite expunge the dazed smile of relief still playing over his features.

"Why?..." he repeated in dismay.

Berger thought he recognized the hoarse voice in the trench which had said "There's a moral problem with volunteers...." Clearly not a peasant.

"We can't leave them up there either."

He was referring to the Russians.

"Has there been an order to withdraw?"

The NCO listened, swaying against a background of apple trees consumed by chancrous mistletoe, his thick lips parted, his eyelids still fluttering violently.

"No more orders," he said at last.

Unable to make any gesture under the heavy body he was carrying, he shook his head as if to convey that orders had vanished forever, together with the entire world.

"What about the officers!" Berger exclaimed.

"I don't know.... They're doing the same as us.... It's not right; man wasn't meant to be putrefied!"

He resumed his laborious march toward the rear. Berger followed.

"If war ... ends up ... like that ..." said the NCO.

He stopped to get his breath. A leaf blew into his open mouth. He spat it out as if he were trying to vomit but could not.

Two soldiers carrying a Russian in a chair formed by their clasped arms came round the edge of the wood. They stopped, and, bending down until their hands touched the glutinous soil, laid down the wounded man. They straightened up with the same relieved smile as the NCO and looked across the dead woods and fields—to reach the field hospital they had to go down toward the river—to the rows of enormous sunflowers nodding in the wind. In the distance, colors still existed, flowers, patches of earth green and tawny, wind-made patterns on the river and on the wide expanse of the valley. The Russian lying stretched out on his back between them made an effort to turn over on his stomach, and finally succeeded. The two Germans had straightened up slowly, spellbound at rediscovering this Promised Land.

Berger dropped his field glasses: his companion, the NCO, was speaking, but not as loudly as his boots, which squelched in the sodden leaves.

"What?" Berger shouted.

The NCO wanted to point at something, but he was holding on to the man on his back by his greatcoat.

"Their boy's sneaking off," he repeated at last.

The high wind billowed through the shirts of the two men who stood stupefied with relief after their exertions; behind them the gassed man was trying to crawl back toward the Russian lines. More than a hundred yards separated him from the wood; after each effort he collapsed again, then resumed his crawl toward his trench, toward the narrow gas-filled ditch in which his comrades lay rotting. But the most inhuman thing was not the sight of this dying man crawling along, his arms up to the elbows in mire, his eyes staring at the mulleins sheathed with swarms of dead insects; it was the silence.

The two gas-masked bearers finally noticed that the Russian had moved away. They caught up with him, one of them booted him in the rump, and then they both hoisted him up onto their clasped arms, set off again, and disappeared.

Berger plunged back into the trees. He should have been going up toward the Russian lines, but each step took him farther away from them. His orders had been not to leave the professor—what professor? He was going back toward the field hospital. He should also have been helping his companion, who was panting with every step under the weight of the dying man, but he neither looked at him nor touched him. Down, down he went through the thickets, arms dangling, staring vacuously at the dead birds lying on the slimy pulp that had once been moss. Yet the enemy trench was no more than three hundred yards away. He kept turning his head toward it, but step by step drew farther away from it.

The path veered toward the German positions. A man was leaping along it on all fours, spastically. Naked. At a distance of two yards, this apparition raised its gray face and whiteless eyes, and parted its lips as if to howl epileptically. Berger drew back. Crazed with pain, and with the twitching movements of a madman, as though its body was nothing but a living torture chamber, with a few froglike leaps the apparition plunged into the putrescent undergrowth.

A howl pierced the prehistoric silence, a howl of utter agony which ended in a whine.

Berger heard once more the noise of a breach being made in those deathly woods.

Above the path some Russian greatcoats were scattered at random, shirts were hanging from the branches as though blasted there by shell bursts; but no trace of an explosion. Close by, in a tiny clearing hidden by a row of sunflowers, some thirty men lay crumpled in a T-shaped trench: an advance enemy post.

They were dead, more or less naked, sprawled on a pile of tattered clothes, clutching one another in convulsive clusters. (Those absurd musings in the sap: the dead stock-still with their cards in the air!) Feet stuck out from the petrified swarm of corpses, toes clenched like fists. No sign of wounds.

Although Berger's hands were still, his right shoulder trembled. His muscles contracted as though his whole body were trying to roll up into a ball; his elbows pressed so violently into his ribs that he could scarcely breathe. Believers, no doubt, call such a visitation of terror the "Presence of the Demon." The Spirit of Evil was even stronger here than death, so powerful that Berger felt compelled to find a Russian, any Russian who had not been killed, hoist him onto his shoulders, and save him.

Five or six of them lay scattered in the bushes, beneath a greatcoat caught by its collar and swinging like a hanged man above this nightmare scene. Berger threw himself at the first one, and, leaning back against the yielding brambles, lifted him up. He was holding a pair of fists like knotted ropes. The man had been floundering among the sunflowers, and a bracelet of one of the huge flat corollas, decomposed by the gas and pierced by a blow, so that it resembled a crown-shaped cake, dangled from his arm. Crown-shaped or wreath-shaped ... a funeral wreath. Berger, with his eyes shut tight, his whole body glued to this fraternal corpse which protected him against all that he was running away from, muttered "Quick, quick, quick," not knowing what he meant and no longer even aware that he was walking. But suddenly he realized that the Russian he was carrying was dead, and dropped him.

He straightened himself up at last. The sunlight struck him despite his closed eyelids. He opened his eyes, and the whole of the upper part of the Russian slope came into view: those long thickets on the side of the hill, corroded and blackened by a final autumn, annihilated by a force as inexorable as the force of Creation, were as nothing beside the face of a single gas victim: in this landscape stricken by a biblical scourge, Berger was aware only of human death. And yet—his eyes were growing accustomed to the sunlight—he felt the dead incandescence quiver as the desert bush quivers with invisible creatures converging on water holes. In the distance he could see white blobs of innumerable shirts in almost parallel lines; from each outcrop of forest, the bearers, their lines crisscrossed by an anthill of fugitives, were descending slowly toward the clearing. What these men were doing Berger now understood—not through any mental process but through the body under whose weight he had sunk up to his knees. Gaping, he watched the assault of pity stumbling down toward the ambulances.

Ahead of him the NCO, whom he had forgotten, was still lumbering on with his Russian. When Berger, with his gas mask raised, caught up with him, he heard him say:

"What's so funny?"

Berger realized that he was roaring with laughter. They walked on in the wind, which was still wafting the gas over to the other side of the ridge.

Although all vegetable matter was dead, not all its shapes had been destroyed; above the grass which had turned to slime, the outlines of brambles and ferns, as well as thistles, were often visible. In the more sheltered spots they were still standing, but the wind, now less laden with leaves, blew them about like bits of charred paper; long brambles like cobwebs crumbled to dust on Berger's tunic, and fell without their thorns catching hold.

"What the devil?" the NCO suddenly said in a strange, questioning voice. He stopped, the entire weight of his body on his left leg, which was sunk in the ooze. The few words he had spoken until then had been spoken into the wind, blurted out as though he were scarcely aware of Berger's presence. This time he turned his face as well as the whole of the Russian's body toward Berger; and yet he still had an "inward" look, his eyes vacant, self-absorbed.

"Hey you! Have you ever eaten bitter almonds?"

"What's the matter? Are you... "

Testing his tongue and the roof of his mouth, the NCO,

suddenly straightening up, frenziedly rid himself of the Russian and stood with his arms outstretched among the windblown brambles and ferns, while the body he had been carrying tumbled to the ground with a soft thud. The Russian came to; Berger heard his breath hissing horribly, and saw his hand clutching the NCO's knee. The latter dragged his boot out of the rotting grass, but the hand did not let go of the green trouser leg.

"I've got three children," the Russian shouted in German.

His other hand was trying to tear at his shirt.

"I've got three children, I've got three..."

The phrase learned by heart, the incantation that was to save him in war. He repeated it feverishly, the words interrupted by a hissing as of punctured bellows, as though his lungs had been perforated. The NCO looked away from him, his eyelids blinking as when he had run across Berger, and furtively dragged away the leg which the other was still clasping.

"And I'm twenty-six years old!" the NCO yelled.

The gassed man did not understand. He had graying hair and the unfinished features of a muzhik. His thick blue lips were moving—speaking; his bluish eyes with their black irises were watching. He did not let go of the trouser leg.

The NCO tore his boot free from the clinging hand and the rotting grass, grazing the gassed man's face, and rushed toward the field hospital as fast as he could go. In front of Berger, figures were plunging through the bushes, all moving, like the NCO, like himself, toward the bright glow of a clearing, from which a voice was carried toward them on the wind:

"... no good ... the other one instead. Over here. Dark blue ... At the end on the left. ..."

Berger made toward this voice, no longer able to run.

"It's mad! Contra-indicated. Blue.... On the left. ..."

At the bottom of the wood a captain was rallying the men, trying to organize the transport of the dying to the field hospital. Medical orderlies in dazzling oxygen masks hurried toward recumbent figures. The professor, also covered with leaves, his muffler flying, his hat pushed back, and his arms flailing like windmill sails, hovered round the captain like a gundog, then rushed to and fro among the casualties. Berger felt the same hatred for the professor that the soldiers had felt for *him* when they encountered him. The professor ran up to him:

"You see! You see! Decisive. Absolutely decisive."

Then he yelled, "No, you fools!" and turned back to Berger (who knew a few words of Russian): "Those fellows over there—that won't do. Tell them at once!"

His dilated pupils scanned the clearing, in which the number of gas victims was increasing.

"Yes, them, those fools drinking!"

They were Russians who had just been laid down beside a stream, and were lapping the water convulsively.

"Contra-indicated! Contra-indicated! Fatal if they drink!"

Seeing the Russians covered with leaves, Berger realized

that he was too, and shook himself without taking his eyes off them.

Nearby, a Russian major, relieved of his oxygen mask, opened his eyes.

"Bring the ambulances up as far forward as possible," the German captain shouted to Berger. "At least one. Plenty of casualties on our side too."

The Germans had taken off their gas masks. It seemed to Berger that he could see only Russians. Unharmed? One of them rushed up, embraced him, pulled a photograph out of his pocket: wife and children. They would pray for him. The Russian was mistaking his savior. Berger heard the motors of the ambulances through the gusts of wind, and hurried toward the sound. The throbbing pain in his knee made him want to vomit. When the wind died down, the noise of the motors faded as if the ambulances were very far away, and in every gap in the foliage, in every opening in the wood, Berger tried to find a vista at the end of which the road would be visible. Emerging from the gas-infected forest, he crossed a wilderness of nettles and burrs and was astounded by their brilliance, their live green, the fine sawtooth leaves of the nettles, the burrs glowing red— so stupefied at seeing colors again that he kept imagining he could see the little splotches of the camouflaged ambulances in the distance. Many of the bramblebushes had already taken on the crimson hue of Virginia creeper; against them the incandescent blue of the harebells and the chicory, the white of the wild carrot, their petals curled back by the gusts of wind, were so intense that his grateful eyelids blinked involuntarily. In that quivering glow of red and blue, the noise of the invisible ambulances grew louder, faded away, started up again, and, suddenly, multiplied by an echo, seemed to be all around him.

At last the noise remained steady through the lulls in the wind; the ambulances were coming up on his left. Berger ran toward them: the motors he heard were not the ambulances but some trucks at the head of a column.

As they passed, first the drivers and then the soldiers stared at him in amazement: belt buckle, hooks, every metal part of his uniform was covered in verdigris. Soon they would be staring at the first gas victim in the same way. Berger also stared at them, one after another: they were going up to the front line, and the barrage of pity would not last indefinitely. Men get used to anything, except dying.

"Have you any ambulances?" Berger shouted to the first NCO.

"Yes, at the rear."

Suddenly Berger felt useless—drained. At his feet blades of grass and their constellations of folioles were outlined in the white dust, and the live thistles thrust up their sturdy spears above all this efflorescence of tiny, quivering reeds. Made of the same light straw, insects flitted among these thin oats, which trembled with the far-off beat of marching boots and were tossed by the wind. Yellow against his uniform still plastered with leaves, a grasshopper landed on Berger's thigh. Just as the gas had merged everything in one and the same putrescence, life was reborn out of a single substance, out of this straw whose hairspring tension activated both the lightest blade of grass and the delicate leap of the grasshopper now vanished into the sun-drenched dust. Over a curtain of trees, the wind soughed with the nautical murmur that it makes through poplars. High above was a great migration of birds.

Berger was not yet released from the moment when he had slung the dead Russian over his back. His shoulders were still haunted by the slithering body; his hands still trembled as at the instant when he had opened them, when that huge sunflower bracelet had disintegrated (and he had glimpsed, directly below him, two hedgehogs, two little brushes with their bristles savagely frizzled by the gas). Was it pity? he vaguely wondered, as he had wondered when he realized that the German troops were retreating; it was a more obscure impulse, in which anguish and fraternity were coupled in the same frenzy. The hillside sloped upward toward the shimmering blue sky, filled with the newfound scent of trees, the scent of boxwood and pine after rain. A large metallic insect flew off, dazzling, burnished—free of verdigris. The murmur of the words overheard in the trench accompanied its buzzing more than the sea-sound of the wind, as it accompanied the troops disappearing round the bend in the road.

Flopping down on the grass, he lit a cigarette. Foul. Another one: same taste. A third. He threw it away: the bittersweet taste persisted. He got up and rushed headlong in the opposite direction from the advancing column, all his strength restored. Was he poisoned? In one crazed instant the dugout and the gas were entangled with the droning voice of the professor under the stars of Bolgako (only yesterday! only yesterday!). What the hell was man doing on this earth! Each time his right foot touched the ground, pain stabbed through his body from his knee to the pit of his stomach, and beneath the whistling of the wind in the branches he could hear distinctly in his throat the thin, hissing, silky sound of his own breath.

Furious at having to slow down on every descending slope, each step a knife thrust into his groin, and with that implacable taste at the back of his nose and throat, he was seized by a realization as peremptory as the thin hissing taking place in his throat: that he had wasted his time, fool that he was, on other things besides happiness. Was that the ambulance? Faster, faster! His legs thrashed the empty air, the whole world suddenly turned upside down, and the forest hurtled into the sky.

He was only half unconscious. He was being carried. Oxygen penetrated his lungs: he had a mask over his face. Euphoria. Consciousness continually on the verge of disappearing. Happiness held no further interest. All these people in snouty masks, denizens of the putrescent forest, and the dead, putrid too. The floor of the trench, with the tarot cards in a ray of kindly sunlight. How strange happiness was. Everything else as well. The dying were said to relive their past. One's life was one's future. Beside him, on a stretcher, a Russian officer was gesticulating: Don't poison me now, not now! and pushing away a gleaming mask. His cries could not drown the sound of breathing that rose in Berger's chest like a foghorn through mist— until he lost consciousness completely....

Part II

Another attack.

It is time for the augurs to forgather.

I was pacing around my study. As though the scene I was describing had pervaded the room, I was overcome by a violent spasm of raging tension, swiveled round with all my strength, hurtled head first against the glass front of the bookcase, hit one of the wooden uprights, and collapsed. The upright did not give; had I deflected the fall which had flung me against the glass? I did not lose consciousness; after the shock, I jotted down, so as not to forget it, the phrase *terrifying possession*. What I was threatened with seemed more like madness than a disease; the word *disease*, which cancer or tuberculosis would evoke, does not spring to my mind when faced with an illness that is unknown to me, especially one from which I suffer no pain. Perhaps madmen do not suffer either.

The word *convulsion* haunts me. Is this because it could be used as the title of the passage I have been reworking for the past ten days? And yet its violence (if not its delirium) has abated. I wanted to add to this narrative the memories it arouses in me today. Before the suspended hand of the gas victims of the City of Death, at an hour which all those men regarded as an hour of destiny, I think of the fresco of Nefertari opposite Luxor: at the entrance to her tomb the wife of Ramses plays against an invisible god of the underworld, whose presence we can only divine from his pawns on the chessboard. Face to face with the void, she stakes her immortality.

My view of man (what else can I call it?) has changed little over the past thirty years. Face to face with death, Major Berger gives happiness an overweening importance; he is young, and if I had taken him out of the field hospital of Bolgako, I should have given him time to reflect.

It is not he who interests me: it is the voice from the depths overheard in the trench, howling or stifled by the silence of the forest.

I wrote the first part of this narrative in prison camp, in 1940. Writing was then the only way to keep alive. So alternately I wrote what the voices in the trench said and noted down what my fellow prisoners said.

Beneath the gray sky still streaked with the slanting smoke trails of burning oil tanks, shadowy figures emerged like selenite prisoners from gigantic pipes left there by some contractor; the rumors went round like wildfire:

"Seems the armistice has been signed. We're being

demobilized, but all the arms factories will have to work against the English. . . ."

"Pétain's been killed by Weygand, in the middle of a cabinet meeting. . . ."

"No, no! Reynaud's in America and Flandin's taken over, with Pétain at the War Office."

"Have you heard! They're taking over seventeen departments! Those Breton bastards are in luck again."

The Bretons, hitherto regarded as "clods," are the objects of general envy: how could Hitler annex Brittany?

"Those autonomists must have been in on the deal!"

"How about us; don't you think we could fix it so's we'd be free Burgundians?"

"The commandant came by just now. I know a bit of German; he said there were a million and a half prisoners."

Laughter all round.

Voices growing ever fainter went on talking about treachery. Faces leaden with hunger and sleeplessness, with a week's growth of beard, watched in silent envy the makeshift cooks toasting their last biscuit or concocting soups like witches' brews. What was beginning to emerge from the resigned and hirsute crowd was not the prison camp but the Middle Ages. What did time matter? They had lived from one day to the next for thousands of years, listening to the same absurd, profound voice.

At night, the rumormongers were silent.

In India, there is morning music and the music "that must be heard at night". . . . On the second evening, in a

Babylonian hovel made of squat pillars, drainpipes, and branches, three crouched Peruvian mummies were writing on their knees.

A pioneer, no longer very young, squatting in the same position but with his arms folded, was staring fixedly at one of the pillars. Sensing that I was watching him, he turned his head slightly:

"Just waiting for it to wear off."

"What?"

"Everything. Just waiting for it to wear off."

It was almost the same phrase the old peasant woman had used, after the tank trap.

When night had finally settled over the camp, a friendly priest confided to me: "All men, at heart, believers or unbelievers, die in a very confused mixture of fear and hope." Next day, the dawn would be aglow with pink fires.

At last, the doctors' conclave. The danger to the cerebellum is confirmed: cure, paralysis, or death. Immediate hospitalization.

The whisper of death alters the appearance of the streets on the way to the Salpêtrière Hospital.

Each change of gear repeats gratingly the word *bizarre*.

I stare at everything I see. As though it had all become very interesting. Self-mockery? Bizarre, simply bizarre and transitory. Even you yourself, transitory.

The Verrières road is almost empty of traffic at ten o'clock in the morning. Thirty years ago it was lined with old houses interspersed with those cement-washed pebble villas on which France had the distressing monopoly. They have now been succeeded by high-rise boxes, and by cranes, those conquering Martians—like Nasser City encroaching on the City of the Dead in Cairo, where in the early morning Cadillacs brush past donkeys with their baskets of dew-drenched jasmine. Fifty years were enough to expunge the traces of Islam, like the fields of the Bible before the eternal desert; to expunge from India the traces of the British empire. In Hong Kong, the typhoons from the south which used to toy with the straw huts now send the bamboo scaffoldings torn from half-finished skyscrapers whirling above the last liners lit up in the harbor. But who cares about Hong Kong? On the road to the Place de Grève condemned men used to smile at the pretty girls. I find it impossible to give a name to the feeling I am experiencing now. Let's say a deferred anguish. Which feeds on everything.

No more fortifications. I remember those of the "Porte d'Allemagne" whence the taxis of the Marne and their pyramids of fezzed spahis set off between the rows of women from the surrounding suburbs lining the streets without a cheer or a song. At my Porte d'Orléans, as in the Place Jean-Jaurès, even the new tenement blocks are incongruous. All shapes are related when the gaze that travels over them may be one's last.

I am entering the Old Quarter of south Paris, whose upper stories belong to Daumier and whose shops, advertisements, and billboards to the world of universal ugliness.

Europe, when I returned to it for the first time, meant shops.

Here is the Gare d'Austerlitz, the bistro which has replaced the luxurious cabaret where Hortense Allart used to sit on Chateaubriand's knee: "I was young, and he used to ask me to sing light songs; and afterwards he did with me what he would. . . ." Here is the Salpêtrière, the ace-of-spades dome of the chapel. My car bounces as it goes under the porch, like the armored Mercedes of the Gestapo as it drove me into Toulouse prison in 1944.

Courtyards, long edifices reminiscent of barracks and palaces: reminders of the past. Then the two clinics, very modern. In the hall, silent figures from a Descent into Hell, mixed with pajama-clad pensioners, furtive wheelchairs.

My room. Two West Indian nurses. One resembles those black mammies who soothed so many infant sorrows during the Creole centuries; the other, tall, cheerful, and handsome, might have been a reincarnation of one of the merry angels of *Green Pastures*. Settling in, dressing gown, corridor: I am conducted to the radiology department. A voice calls for help from the elevator, which is stuck between two floors. Another elevator. Another corridor. Horrible little trolleys, stretchers—from one of which an arm dangles in the age-old posture of dead heroes. An astonishing silence: one expects groans or screams. The nurse ushers me in. The consultant is cordial. Assorted apparatus.

Back to my room. The X-ray room was white-enameled, the corridor was white-enameled, my room is white-enameled. The flowers sent by my friends look out of place in this world devoid of wood or fabric, as alien as a planet on which only white paint, nickel, test tubes, glass objects, sheets—and invalids—could survive. I have been in bed for only a quarter of an hour when a doctor comes in, an old friend who resembles the General de Gaulle of 1940, at the time of his oak-leaved kepi: "There's nothing irreversible." Which means, I suppose, that the cerebellum has not yet been affected. A verdict of life?

Do they ever pronounce the other one?

... Military hospital in Madrid during the first days of the revolution, a cellar in which the aquarium glow from the skylights overgrown with ferns gave a leaden hue to the El Greco faces of the amputated militiamen; in 1945, wards prepared for our soldiers of the Ill and the Rhine who were suffering from frostbite after the river crossing (and who were to be saved by Dr. Jacob, thanks to the supplies of Leriche serum preserved in Strasbourg). So many Alsatian hospitals with blood everywhere, the blood that is absent here. ...

The clatter of plates and forks subsides, and night falls. In spite of the soundproofing, cries of pain, which I recognize because they all sound like the cries of children, echo through the corridors when the door opens. Cries of patients sunk in pre-coma, who feel nothing, according to the nurse: when they recover, all they can remember is having fallen asleep. "Not true," one of the consultants told me sadly. "We know little about what happens in pre-coma: patients who have recovered sometimes quote back to us things we said in their presence during their catalepsy." Poor nurse! Those who have to live amid the murmur of pain need to ignore it.

The drip solution which immobilizes me is to last for twelve hours. The needle quivers in the vein in my arm. No more light under my door; nothing but the to-and-fro of the night nurses—and, each time they enter, the distant cries unconsciously uttered by those who will recover and those who will not. Crouching like Fates, unconsciousness and death have taken possession of the Salpêtière.

Once more I am disconcerted by the absence of pain. Death, in our minds, is so powerfully linked with pain that we are stunned by an illness which may be mortal but which does not torture us—dumbfounded by the most disconcerting divorce of our time. Death hovers over hospitals in an insidious, biological way unknown on the battlefield. Here, the sick succeed one another like generations upon the earth. But these generations do not recover.

The importance I have always attributed to the metaphysical character of death has made people believe that I am obsessed by mortality. One might as well believe that biologists devoted to the study of birth are looking for jobs as wet nurses. Death is not to be confused with my own demise.

Mourning is becoming extinct, children are kept away from cemeteries, but on television a day without a murder would be a day without bread. The act of dying is linked with violence. I remember Saint-Exupéry's surprise when I said to him one day: "Physical courage is nurtured by a sense of invulnerability." I never thought of death during any aerial dogfight or when my plane was being shot at by anti-aircraft batteries. *Nothing would happen*—although an anti-aircraft barrage brays like a donkey: the plane *can* be shot down! To see the tank in front of yours blown up by a mine is not encouraging either. At Gramat, I did not believe that the firing squad was going to shoot at me—and they did not shoot, but if they had been given the order to do so I should have gone on believing they wouldn't until they opened fire. When, later, I found myself surrounded by mortar fire, I didn't think it was funny nor did I believe that the next shell would hit me; yet mortar shells come whining over closer and closer as if seeking you out, and my Sam Browne belt had just been slashed by shrapnel. I have felt threatened, not by the sound of bullets, but by the fall of my wounded comrades. I have had a few serious illnesses—and waited until they were over. When the anesthetists put me under, I have never been afraid of not waking up again. In illness as in battle, I have never even felt the wonderment at life that I feel today—although I have sometimes felt it after the event, as at Bône after my safe landing: the glove-maker's sign, an enormous red hand above the ill-lit shop at nightfall, and the motionless dog in the furrier's window. As for suicide, I have been shot at enough to be capable of shooting myself. No doubt fear often comes from imagining wounds in the stomach or the genitals; I imagine nothing. I don't suffer from vertigo, that's all. But here I am living with the dying, not with fighting men.

Illness is oblivious of the lure of danger. In my case, at least; for at my dead father's bedside. . . .

During the 1914–18 war he often lodged with the priest when he returned from the front. He had the absent-minded faith of so many men of his generation: memories of church, my mother's example, a vague deism. In each new presbytery he would interrogate a new priest: "Of course I believe in God; but our Arabs, and the Hindus, the Buddhists, the Jews also believe in him; and if I believe in Jesus Christ, isn't it simply because I learned my cate-chism?" The replies varied, and did not convince him any more than had Pascal. When he killed himself, he left a book on his bedside table open at a page on which he had underlined the words: *And who knows what we shall find after death?* Curiosity for the unknown had insinuated itself into the stoical shade of the suicide.

Phenomenologies of religions were nonexistent. The best would not have operated more powerfully than Pascal. What role does thought play in this domain? I lost my faith after my Confirmation. And later, my agnosticism was accompanied not so much by meditations, which dried up at the age of twenty, as by the religious ceremonies of Asia, as if destiny embodied my father's simple questioning in terms of spectacle. The faith of multitudes is pervasive. Not that it convinces, but the faith of Asia was impressed upon me in the Pamirs, at dawn upon the shoreless ocean, or under a star-studded desert sky. "An immense blessedness descended from the firmament," Victor Hugo says of biblical times. I have heard the call rising up from thousands of bodies prostrated in prayer in the courtyard of the world's largest mosque, in Lahore, and it was echoed from every mosque rising up between Timbuktu and the confines of the Gobi Desert in the solemn self-abandonment of Islam. The same call went up from the throng of pilgrims in the sanctuary where Buddha spoke to the gazelles, from the profusion of yellow gladioli bowing together in the joined hands of the women in the pagoda at Rangoon.

I remember the coach museum in Lisbon. Not just a garage, like the one there used to be at Versailles, but a real museum, inhabited by its coaches as the palace of Versailles is inhabited by its furniture. In the middle of them is a curious black carriage, a single-seat gig, rather like a rickshaw, which could be enclosed by an oilcloth curtain in front of the occupant when the evening downpour began. The occupant was a coffin; this phantom vehicle is called the Death Coach. "Always with a black horse, senhor," said the curator.

Pain waits for nightfall at the Salpêtrière. During the daytime there are drip solutions, injections, comings and goings of Green Pastures preceded by her laugh, other nurses who want to chat until the moment comes when I am able to answer them, tomorrow, the day after.... Although I am in little pain, I am far away, withdrawn into my fever. The mind surrenders itself to the groping fingers of death as it does to those of sleep.

Once the dinner plates and glasses cease to clatter, the door will not open again except for the visit of the night nurse. The silence with which I am growing familiar descends, filled with its teeming moans, as the silence of a tropical forest descends in the moonlight over the murmur of plants and wakeful insects.

Ten o'clock. The desolation of the Italian child whom I hear calling "Mama" above me every quarter of an hour echoes the cries of the night birds in the Siamese forest, the ululation of monkeys at dawn. Hospitals are haunted, but the exhaustion of the patients accords with the irresistible assuagement of the dark. What do the Buddhists call it? Yes: the Peace of the Abyss.

The days slip by. Released from the drip solution, I can walk as far as the window. In the courtyard, the doctors' and visitors' cars seem to be guarded by walking cripples. Is there nothing left on this earth but invalids? The unreality is reinforced by a jolly nurse whom I secretly call Moulinette, since I do not know her name, and who says to me: "Ah, you young rascal!" The whole thing is like a dream, encouraged by the sleeping pills. But there is also reality. A new patient has been put into the room next to mine. At six o'clock in the evening he snored loudly. "We must transfer him to another room," one of the nurses says to me. I expostulate: "If the patients can't put up with one another, who will put up with them?" Alas, I think I recognize those snores: they will turn into a death rattle.

The murmuring of pain gradually starts up in the silence of the night, punctuated by this wheezing, regular and calm.

How can one become accustomed to an intolerable wait? For twelve days I have waited for the doctors' decision; since I came here, I have been waiting, while scribbling illegible notes, for the treatment to take effect, or to fail. If I am to die this time, will dying have consisted of waiting? We think of illnesses as dramas; sometimes they are somnolences—somnolences from which one does not awaken.

The unconscious is an attentive collaborator. I correct my phrase, for I had written simply "If I die"—as if death were a hypothesis.

The hot sheets of the daily fever muddle everything. To take my mind off the plaintive murmuring, I try to sort these images into a desultory chronology. The approach of summer, with the cockchafers alongside a row of acacias; the first whiff of the invisible sea; the fear of gypsies; the evening when the discovery of the palace of Versailles is mixed up with the memory of a shrew, like a tiny kangaroo, which hopped across the forest road to dodge my father's little car; my return from the house in the Ardennes to the station at Rethel: cattle asleep on their feet on that August night of 1914, and a squadron of lancers with gleaming lances sweeping across the fields. The snowstorm in which the train was held up all night at the beginning of the battle of Verdun; the shadowy figure encountered in a Métro entrance who muttered to me as he went by, like a password: "The armistice is signed!"

Late summer 1939. In the Place de l'Oeuf in Montpellier, the moving strip of illuminated news headlines follows the circular promenade of evening strollers who grow more and more numerous. They have just read the announcement of the German-Soviet pact. The parched smell of summer fills the square. In words that flicker like rows of fireflies beneath the importunate stars, Death spells out the illuminated message THE REICH DEMANDS A CONDOMINIUM FOR THE FRENCH AND BRITISH COLONIES. France's war has begun.

The retreat through the dahlias and the last of the wisteria, the whole sky streaked with the smoke trails of oil tanks in flames; the muffled clatter of the last train receding into the distance: *you are pri-son-ers, you are pri-son-ers.*

Dawn rising day after day above the fires, the giant chimney pipes and the barbed wire of the camp. The day of my escape, every tree as menacing as if Germans were hidden behind each trunk; my shoes, which are too small for me, emulating the torture of the boot; the film on the taking of Warsaw in the cinema in whose darkness I take refuge between trains: the seething plumes of smoke turn into a tranquil sea of clouds traversed by the aircraft, beneath which cities blaze and the roads fill with the immemorial stream of fugitives.

The cat that follows me to the edge of the forest, intriguing the German sentries, while I cross the demarcation line, on my fortieth birthday.

Roquebrune, the sound of my son's little clogs in the

garden where the Judas trees are in flower (and I remember thinking that was what my heartbeats would sound like when I was dying).

Does one really see one's life unreel before one when one loses consciousness as a result of an accident? Marcel Arland once told me that he had experienced this vertiginous film. I myself have never experienced it, either in aerial combat or in front of the firing squad at Gramat. Does it only occur at the last gasp? (Arland had nearly drowned.) I am provoking a sort of vague self-defense, and know it. For the purposes of these *Anti-Memoirs,* I have developed the habit over the past few years of seizing and storing up the images of the past. Those that succeed each other here come pat—a biography as false as any other. Are they oriented toward war because of the death rattle from the next room? Here once more is the whirl of lancers among the sleeping cattle. The imagery revolves as the wooden horses in the Spanish merry-go-round continued their musical cavalcade through the solitude of the bombardment. The death rattle, its plaintive wheeze now more intermittent, thinks for me. I remember the dead siestas of the civil war, the bitter cold of the Ebro, a goat, crazed by an air raid, butting open the revolving door of the Bank of Spain, a return from a bombing mission over Teruel, guided by the blue glow of the bonfires of dried oranges, with one of the pilots killed, and the rising sun on the face of the rear gunner. What memory mutters Napoleon's phrase "The most painful courage is the courage of three o'clock in the morning"? Airfields in the small hours before the departure of the bombers, and, years later, all of us crouching in the fields of Dannemarie in the hoarfrost faintly reddened by the glow of blazing farms.

At least I know where *these* images come from: a clock strikes three.

From time to time the mind intervenes, tentatively. But the proximity of death does not encourage self-examination; it repels it. Men and women here who talk about their lives simply say that they have or have not been "lucky." What would a self-examination be if it were not an examination of "conscience"? Of wonder? Wherever death prowls, it is the sole object of wonderment. I think of all those who have spoken to me about their lives, pretending to address me when they were first and foremost addressing themselves. My father, shortly before his suicide: "If I am to have another life, I want none other than my own." Drieu,* in a letter. Above all Méry, when he recalled the long procession of women in his life. A film star has since remarked to me: "You've no idea what the memory of their first lover is for most women. It's a memory that never dies."

Nighttime in Singapore, smelling of asphalt, pepper, and China. The tall silhouette of the disillusioned centurion played with the Cambodian child, who was playing with the cat, Pen-wiper.... He said, speaking of the Street of Death: "Before it disappears, or I disappear ..." It has been

* Pierre Drieu la Rochelle (1893–1945): novelist, poet, and literary/political journalist. Committed suicide in 1945 after being charged with collaboration with the Germans during the occupation. (Tr.)

demolished. Then he said—and I could tell from his voice that he was smiling in the darkness: "I'm hurrying patiently toward death.... Oh no, I really have no wish to sign on again...."

He spoke to me of the military band that used to play Verdi in the square at twilight in Phnom Penh for the French pierrots in white linen and the pierrettes in printed muslin—during colonial days. And of the end of Indochina: "It was the time of the Mad Bonze, the founder of the Hoa-Hao ... when rice was flung into the wind for errant souls...." The footsteps of a nurse in the Salpêtrière mingles with the squelch of bare feet on the tiled floor of the veranda during the rainy season. With weary bitterness Méry talked of the women he had loved, and his slow, languid voice echoed mockingly in the stillness of the Malayan night, broken by the bark of a single dog. "I should like to confide in death, which is not far away: what luck for humanity to understand nothing about anything!"

Understand what? replies the death that surrounds me. We do not question our own identity. "The self, that incomparable and elusive monster that each of us cherishes in his heart," I wrote in *Man's Fate* forty years ago.

The plaintive murmur starts again (does it start at the same hour in every hospital throughout the world?).

Illnesses of which one dies are called mortal illnesses. What should we call illnesses of which one *might* die? A disease that has a name only for the doctors seems an enigma when it is divorced from pain, which has a name for everyone. Faced with this amorphous threat, my most constant feeling is astonishment. For in this pain-haunted place I am still in no pain. A sudden bout of Chinese flu, as intrusive as a cat in a cemetery, has thrown the diagnostic observations out of gear. With the aid of a stick I can walk to the far end of the corridor, where there is a window looking onto the courtyard. For the first time, down there among the cars, I see my fellow patients in a group. I had glimpsed them on my arrival, and I never go to the radiology room without passing wheelchairs and stretchers with dangling arms. Seven years ago—only seven years—not one of us would have come out of here intact. Down there, pajama-clad figures wander around with walking sticks, wheelchairs, or walkers, and, when one of them turns round, the face of sickness. It is our Street of Death. Striped pajamas, shades of the extermination camps liberated in 1945. The enemy is not the ephemeral Reich, but paralysis, which is as old as man.

Of course, there is suicide.

In Spain, at Gramat, on the Rhine, death was closer. There, it belonged only to fate; here, it also belongs to me. The takeoff of the aircraft, the parachute jump—"Out we go, and we'll see what happens!"—with the same elusive chance in which one firmly believes: a safe landing, and here, a cure.

Or not.

I have always been surprised by what people have written about suicide. The preposterous need to turn it into an offense, or a value. Man, born for death, is born to choose his death if he so wishes. By all means let others' lives be sacrosanct (how seldom they are!); but not mine. One of my characters in *The Royal Way* quoted the remark of an adventurer famous in Indochina: "There is no such thing as death; there is only me, who is about to die...." The importance of the self is in decline.

Death by hemlock was a privilege; Socrates did not suffer. We know a great deal about hemlock, in all its varieties. The ancient texts tell us that some of them were painless. What Western specialist has studied their effects? Analyses now as simple as those that isolated morphine would give man mastery over his own life.

At the risk of proffering him death. Too high a price.

I am not forgetting Méry's perplexity: "How is it possible that no civilization—not one!—has allowed men to choose their own death.... As though it weren't enough not to be able to choose to be born!" Although bravery is common in military civilizations, was common in the Foreign Legion, at Verdun, at Stalingrad. But all such courage is lit by the red glow of lotteries. The irremediable is not a lottery.

Or is it? What about the book my father was reading?

"Always death," Méry used to say, "but not always the same death...." The Vedic moon was reflected in the little pond in the patio, and women in evening dress flitted across the light. He spoke of what he called his "destiny" with astonishment more than anything else. Five years ago. Now he is dead.

"If you are a knight, die like a knight!" ordains the *Bhagavad-Gita*. The cosmic life of Hinduism is heedless enough of individual life to hide death under the mantle of duty to the State. Christendom, although its doctrine associated death with the Last Judgment, nonetheless serenely conceded it to the "dangerous occupations." Its knights were no less intrepid than the Kchatriyas.* Or the plebeians of the Year II, or the Bolsheviks of October: duty to the State reincarnated. For me, the right to commit suicide is an intrinsic State right—or State duty? And besides, what is one to make of suicide—a whole world!— when one has spent a year and a half clinging to a *protective* cyanide pill?

The doctors in this hospital maintain as a working hypothesis that we have retained inside our brain another, prehominoid, brain which is the legacy of some Plesiosaurian ancestor; only one of our two brains accepts death. It is true that we speak of suicide with an intelligence worthy of saurians. But the hostility it inspires is often accompanied by an unconscious solidarity with misfortune. As if suicide were a betrayal of all the sick and the halt, all the unfortunates who have not killed themselves. Human fellowship, like courage, chooses its moments. Tonight, I shall be less firm and far less lucid. Plesiosaur or not, I know what I shall think if I think of

* Consecrated Hindu warriors. (Tr.)

72

those poor derelicts of life, for I know that I should not dare kill myself in front of them.

Return of the flu. Temperature one hundred and four degrees at first; then the fever subsides, and I wrap myself in its warmth and in daydreams. Once more Singapore, the mist, the barking dog. "What have I to do with that child in the hood?"—and the Cambodian child stroking Penwiper. And I, what have I got to do with ... what? My memory never focuses on myself without an effort. I have read what concerns my books, not what concerns me. I do not remember my childhood. Nor even, without deliberate concentration, the women I have loved or thought I loved, or my dead friends. Could I recall, even if I applied my mind to it, three of my birthdays? Someday, perhaps (if someday comes) I shall make a study of the mechanisms of memory, which have always intrigued me. Psychoanalysis retains only its "content"; yet the aptitude for happy memories does not orient man toward the same pole as the aptitude for hostile memories. Did Freud ever write the word *happiness?* When I am able to speak to my fellow patients, I shall ask them if their memories are often linked to the elements: clouds, river currents, the night.... On the evening of my seventeenth birthday, I am crossing the Pont du Châtelet, and the emotion of the *Oresteia* which I have just discovered in the theater in Leconte de Lisle's version mingles with the twilight behind the black towers of the Trocadéro.... Or if those memories are linked as much to what pertains to life in general as to our own life. "My memories group themselves according to heat and cold," Hemingway once told me.

During another conference among the doctors, in the radiology department, I glanced through the illustrations in a book about me. The photographs of me as a child, as a schoolboy, as a soldier, as a minister, as a passerby express my life even less than the succession of those who accompany me therein. The black cat that trailed me to the edge of the wood does not follow upon the black towers of the Trocadéro in the twilight, or even my escape. The mountain ridge that divides the two versants of Malaya stretching down to the Indian Ocean on one side and to the Pacific on the other does not follow upon my memory of the Himalayas, lost in the mist that shrouded the upper range; the Malayan coolies do not follow upon the Tibetan women porters, sticking out their tongues as a sign of welcome, on the platform of the little station. Images do not make up a life story; nor do events. It is the narrative illusion, the biographical work, that creates the life story. What did Stendhal pin down, except a few moments of his? Each of us articulates his past for the benefit of an impalpable interlocutor: God, in the confessional; posterity, in literature. One has no life story except for others. I began to remember my past in 1941, sitting in front of the fire in my house at Roquebrune. It was a long time since I had seen logs blazing in a fireplace, and I thought, Is it age knocking at the door for the first time? The images here arrange themselves by analogies: lances in the Ardennes and at Djibouti, blind men in Montmartre and in the dark night of Spain, the dog in the window at Bône and the cat that accompanied me to the demarcation line, fires flickering with gesticulating shadows in the fields of the Resistance, and so many airfields at dawn...

Once more I hear above me the cry "Mama!" The groans from the neighboring room have become louder, clearly distinguishable from all the others. There is no longer the shadow of a doubt: it is a death rattle.

Myself. Inexplicably this personage, which sometimes obsesses me, does not interest me here. My body, with its temporary cells, is mine, and if I poison myself it is I and no other who will die; and yet a world like ours, where divorce is widespread, suggests the discontinuity rather than the continuity of the individual. "I've always admired Goethe," Méry used to say; "I'm no longer very convinced that the accidental transforms itself into experience—or that I'm remotely connected with the insufferable adolescent in a hood that I once was." Nevertheless he remembered that adolescent, in a way that was peculiar to him. My past is an encumbrance to me. On my fortieth birthday (when I was crossing the demarcation line clandestinely with the black cat), I wished I had been born the day before. Our civilization, in which the moment has become king, treats the past as death does. Man. Man is the voices of the French prisoners in the camp, the voices of the German soldiers in the trench. And what is a past when it is not a life story? An awareness of existing, which is deeper than consciousness, and which I do not regard as cognition?

I have reread the account of Antoine's death in *Les Thibault*. Roger Martin du Gard, anxious for documentary exactitude, lived among doctors. For a long time Antoine hopes to recover. I find his sentiments surprising. If I die here, will people speak of a strange death? I do not find myself drawing up a balance sheet of my life, any more than I see my past flash dizzily by as drowning people do. I feel no pangs at the thought of what will disappear with me. Few memories of feelings, not even love. No litany of "never again." A sense of the lightning speed of the past; scarcely any sense of duration. Images, not events, unless I search for them. A consciousness without memory. Indifference to the idea of having to decide on the moment for suicide ("To say to oneself: tonight..." Antoine anxiously notes; he *does* kill himself). One can think of suicide at leisure, I know; condemned Roman patricians were in no hurry. Would Socrates have shown himself less patient if he himself had chosen death—which he at least accepted? One can also kill oneself straightaway.

I once wrote: "What do I care about what matters only to me?" Egoism only tends to make us prefer ourselves, with a muddled vehemence. Have I thought about myself a great deal? Self-approval does not really demand it. Nor the opposite, after all: men are not much given to finding fault with themselves. I shall not begin to do so tonight. "One must know men in order to influence them" is twaddle. What about knowing oneself? Important decisions are like rabbits one shoots at in passing; far better to know how to shoot straight. We are inhabited by banal monsters. Thought without action as its object we call meditation, and this word is not far removed from prayer. After which, "to philosophize is to learn how to die." An ambitious phrase, at the Salpêtrière. Its grave resonance does not respond to "Who am I?" but with "What is a life?"

The death rattle has begun again.

I know nothing of my next-door neighbor. A man. An unknown life. Unknown except to himself. Perhaps not even that. It was Rousseau, I think, who had the temerity to fill the vacuum left by the ebb tide of Christian universalism with his own life and his discovery of "nature" ("I've discovered butterflies and nature with the approach of death," Méry told me). I know what an artist can glean from the endless dialogue of the sun and the ocean; I know the meaning of the play of shadows around the funeral pyres, the ashes floating down the Ganges by night in the blue and red coruscations of its waters. I know, Jean-Jacques, what a great mind can extract from an herbal; and also that a Zen monk seeks to divine the growth of a blade of grass without seeing it. But at the hour when the city awakens with the faint, deep whine of the shingle in the bays, the loudest voice is not the voice of death which surrounds me and which I carry within me, but the mystery of life beneath which men burn themselves out or pass away—as Warsaw in flames melted away in the film, shrouded in the white serenity of the sea of clouds. My awareness of my life as it hangs in the balance is an inchoate but ineluctable response, like the awareness of equilibrium revealed at the instant in which we lose it. The ultimate awareness has nothing in common with the memory of our actions or the unveiling of our secrets. One is not one's own life history for oneself. Asia has always sensed that man's cardinal problem is to grasp "something else." The nocturnal pyres reflected in the Ganges awaiting the call of destiny like our maquis fires awaiting the airplanes from London, the Buddha made phosphorescent on attaining Enlightenment, while a flock of migrant birds wheels above him.... Death whispers to me, today as on my escape from the tank trap, that the secret of our life would be no less poignant if man were immortal.

The nurse comes in, hypodermic at the ready. "Don't be afraid," she says, with an unnecessary laugh, for I no longer feel injections. Those words are no doubt part of her stock-in-trade. She leaves. The sounds of pain rise with the day. From the moment of my departure from Verrières the streets had seemed to me bizarre; nurses and doctors seem bizarre too, and the plants left on my windowsill in violation of the rules. There are some cyclamens, and I like their fleshy petals, just as I like the texture of mushrooms. A Japanese once told me: "If you looked at flowers in the same way as you look at cats, you would have an honorable understanding of Life." It is Life that is bizarre, and when the wooden carousel horses of memory revolve, it is my life. My cat flew across the drawing room and then stopped, its paws stretched out, licking itself meticulously: it had changed its mind. Dreams of cats, destinies of plants... Each form of life seems bizarre to the rest, like the road from Verrières, but all of them together seem bizarre to ... to whom, to what? Were religions created in order to bring men gods to whom they would not be bizarre?

On Shakespeare's "tale told by an idiot, full of sound and fury, signifying nothing" the wretched little pile of secrets cannot have imposed its paltry meaning for long. "What does life mean?" remains the most tenaciously persistent question. I think of Benares, of General de Gaulle. He is dead now.... Looking out at the snow-covered fields of St. Bernard, I had said to him, and he had repeated: "Why should life have a meaning?"

The proximity of the death throes of others drowns the question "What am I?," makes it otiose. Would it be untrue of a solitary death struggle? This tourist trip through the archipelago of death disregards any sequence of events, lays bare only the most inchoate and most intense consciousness, the convulsive "I am." But not beyond the other question: What is human destiny? The snow of Colombey, the snow of the Vézère... During the winter of 1943, between illustrious Les Eyzies and unknown Lascaux, where our weapons were hidden, I wondered to myself, as I thought of the distant herds of reindeer in the prehistoric snows, if man was born when for the first time he murmured "Why?" at the sight of a corpse. He has repeated himself a great deal ever since. Inexhaustible brute.

There is a knock at the door. A stranger comes in without waiting for an answer. A white mouse with white hair.

"Forgive me for disturbing you, monsieur. I know you

are a very learned man, and besides ... they don't hide
things from you so much. I'm your new neighbor, and I
thought we might perhaps ... Well, the point is: people
often die here."

I answer, not without a certain uneasiness:

"Not nowadays."

"Ah, do you think so? Not nowadays? Not nowadays.... I don't want to disturb you ... I'm going."

He bows, in little jerky movements.

"Anyhow, in my case, if ever ... that is ... if ever, they
can be sure that I shall know how to behave: I shan't
bother anyone. Thank you, monsieur. I think you've
reassured me a little."

I have been sent a charming toy cat, which meows when
you press its stomach. Its name is Furry. The West Indian
nurses come and stroke it, delighted to see a cat in the
clinic, even a toy one. Its presence reminds me of the
Gestapo men who played leapfrog under the vaulted
arcades of the prison in Toulouse. But poor Furry is not
much protection. Is the sharp rise in my temperature due
to the intense but spasmodic Chinese flu or to a relapse?
Imprisoned by it, I wander from one memory to another
and see the toy cat wandering from one piece of furniture
to another. Images of Spain begin to whirl around once
more. The girl I met again in Madrid whom I had loved in
Siberia when the lights of the Soviet factories shone out
across the steppes like the hope of the world. Mao, as
massive and powerful as the absurd Egyptian column of the
People's Palace against which he leans, with his nurse

behind him. A bygone war: an old man, tottering like the Chinese empire, fleeing through the bombs clutching to his chest a cricket in a cage. In a restaurant courtyard, a banana tree glitters above a transparent coral like an enormous flowering peach tree: the heaped shells of crayfish. A church bell rings. (Isn't the Salpêtrière chapel deconsecrated?) What did the first church bell sound like in its wooden Merovingian bell tower? Where will the last one ring? Beside the heaped corpses of an extermination camp, their backs bristling with vertebrae, a survivor being interviewed by a journalist fingers his getup, which resembles the pajamas of the patients here, and replies with all the voice that remains to him: "You see, there's no room left in our hearts except for forgiveness." Trains in the rain. Assurbanipal's inscription: "The voices of men, the tread of cattle and sheep, the glad shouts of rejoicing I banished from the fields, and the wild beasts made their home there." Wild beasts—I know the region of Babylon— in herds on the sands of the desert that murmur like the sand in an hourglass, as the murmur of pain begins to stir around me now. Night is falling. The hum of activity, the clatter of supper trays, the plaintive chorus are on the way, as, around the beleaguered maquis strongholds, the noises of the night rose with the cries of awakened animals, growls of the invisible war, and approach of the invisible enemy. Moulinette's face, Green Pastures' laugh.

I wake up. Night has fallen. "Don't hurt me!" cries my poor neighbor, whom the nurse has failed to reassure. They have let me go on sleeping. I often sink imperceptibly into sleep. Although I am still in little pain, I feel a sort of all-enveloping dizzy nausea, ready to burst, as though I were about to vomit. The tablets I am supposed to take have been left in the bathroom. I go to fetch them without switching on the light, and return toward my bed, which is very high, like all hospital beds. I feel along the wall. No switch. I sink to the floor in the black fog, painlessly, my legs like cotton wool. A coolness: have I fallen on the tiles? The bed should be opposite me. I cannot get up; cannot even move. Not only am I floundering in the darkness like a drowning man, I do not even know where I am. There are no bearings. Nothing is more difficult to describe than an unknown sensation. Our bearings are almost as much a part of us as our limbs; my body has disappeared with them: no more body, no more "I," nothing surrounding me, an agonized consciousness which does not suggest the approach of death, although it is not the consciousness of normal life. The darkness drifts. I manage to turn round and crawl on all fours toward the bed. Shall I be able to pull myself up by the sheets, and find the light switch or the bell push? I have advanced three feet; my hand touches a surface. It is not the bed but a wall—which moves. An "attraction" at Luna Park long ago as a child: wedged in a seat, I saw the little room heave up and turn upside down around me. Later, more menacingly, the moment when the falling aircraft emerged from the clouds to find the earth tilting beneath it. Is it an attack? Of what?

Here is the bed. It seems much smaller. Very hard. An object falls from it and breaks. Why have they put glass objects on my bed? And how narrow it is! I must not fall.

Have I lost consciousness? Before my arrival at the clinic, when I fell I remained conscious. The darkness no longer revolves. Gradually I reemerge. It is not my bed. I can place my feet on the cool tiles and skirt round the thing on which I have been lying; once more I am in a void, a darkness without shapes or bearings, in which my weight pulls me down toward the floor. My left hand touches a flat surface; I kneel down. I do not know where I am, but the tiles hurt my knees, and the flat surface is certainly a wall. I try to raise myself up, succeed in doing so at the third attempt, come across another wall. Still no bed. Can I have gone blind? Luckily, though the darkness is intense, it is uneven. I grope my way leftward. A piece of furniture; a lamp falls; it is the bedside table. I touch the bed—and then, the light switch!

Here is the white-enameled room, with the flowers on the windowsill. I realize that I must have walked to the right thinking that I was walking straight ahead, and that I curled up on a low table; a plane surface. Here is my real bed—in which my predecessor perhaps died, in which illness awaits my successor—and which I left twenty-five minutes ago, according to my bedside clock.

And the tablets? The bottle gleams over by the wall, in the opposite corner. I have been right round the room. While I was unconscious? I do not remember having fainted. Does one remember? I am reminded of what the doctor told me about his patients after they recovered from pre-coma. These twenty-five minutes of somnambulistic life under the threat of death do not disturb me as a blackout but as an hallucination. Fainting means nothing to me: I have fainted only once, when I was twelve. Fainting, like being put under for an operation, suggests sleep; before stretching out on the table, I was not asleep, far from it. . . .

In the corridor, the moans have started again.

So I went right round the room. . . . I have always associated dying with the death throes, and am stupefied by this anguished feeling in which I discern only the unknown threat of finding myself cut off from the earth.

Neither pain, nor memory, nor amnesia—nor dissolution. Loss of consciousness, but not of *all* consciousness. I thought I was in another part of the room, but somewhere; I could not understand what had become of my bed, but I tried to stretch out on it, to settle down in my litter: must try and get to sleep; it will all be clear tomorrow. I remember the effort I made. Can one conceive of Lazarus remembering his efforts to settle into his tomb?

Without being conscious of it, except in retrospect, I experienced something of which I have had a presentiment ever since my arrival at the Salpêtrière: an "I" without a self; a life without an identity. The madman assumes one. To lose one's identity suggests losing everything; I did not dissolve into nothingness, because my consciousness took refuge in my exertions. An animal consciousness? A sleepwalker conscious only of the intensity of his effort to reach the roof, and who retains the memory of it?

Man, as I have said, is the quintessence of the voices that

filled the trench and the prison camp. It has been said that man is the sum of his fantasies, his drives, his hidden desires. I am tempted to write that man is what is built on that consciousness which is so passionately determined to exist, simply to exist; but are they not inextricably bound to one another like the plinth to the statue? Why should I be interested in this amoeba-like creature? Because of what it has in common with myself, with the self of dreams and the madman: the consciousness of effort.

What fascinates me about my adventure is the walk atop the wall between life and the boundless depths foretokening death. It is also the memory of those depths. "The resuscitated remember nothing" (except conversations between doctors!). An encounter with the part of man that walks, whimpers, or yells when consciousness is no longer there.

I was conscious of no longer knowing where I was—of having lost touch with the earth. No pain except the pain of others, which beats faintly against the walls of this white room where the little night-light glows, as the muffled roar of the ocean could be heard beating against the shore from my room in Bombay. My mind is lucid, but its activity is limited to the endless recollection of a nowhere land, the amazed contemplation of a state hitherto unknown. What happened bears no relation to what I used to call dying.

Where does that subdued hubbub come from? I see no sign yet of the gray light of dawn. No sound of breakfast trays; in any case the noises seem to be coming from the ground, and I recognize the heavy footsteps of the male nurses who take patients to the radiology room. The steps recede, and the door of the adjacent room closes on hollow silence. I no longer hear those loud moans. The male nurses were not going to the X-ray room: my neighbor is dead.

I am awakened by the real daylight. I remember something that actually happened, not a nightmare at all. Yet memories are stimulated by what resembles them, and this panic resembles no other. I lost my bearings—as in my study; but I have returned from a terrifying limbo, not from the void, and from the incommunicable, not from chaos. Nothing in common with hashish and its whirling of great wings. Nor with the sleep of the operating table. I have experienced a sensation as utterly new to me as the first sexual sensation, as the taste of water once, in Tashkent, when, maddened with thirst, I heard my leathery tongue striking the roof of my mouth with a noise like a wooden clapper.

As I continue to note down what has happened to me, I am reminded of what my friend Raja Rao, the Indian writer who was my interpreter with Nehru, once told me:

"Westerners, and they are not alone in this, believe that there exists one room, which is life, and another, which is the beyond, and that death is the door through which we pass from one to the other. Isn't this so? Why do they dramatize the door? Death is the path to Enlightenment. You know this when you come back from it—or at least from something like it. My guru used to go into a trance for several hours, and come back. The Buddha experienced Enlightenment well before dissolving into it. One can choose one's death. Indirectly: Gandhi had predicted that he would be assassinated. Or even directly. Have you ever heard this story in Europe? The police arrest a gang of highway robbers. One of them is quite unlike the others. He impresses the police so much that they separate him from the rest and heighten the wall surrounding his cell. After some months a young man arrives with influential references, and asks to see the prisoner. They are taken to the visiting room, where they are separated by a grille, as in your country, I believe. The young man prostrates himself. The prisoner tells him to rise and asks, "Why have you come so late?" There are explanations and questions from the young man. The voices are lowered; the wardens hear the names of divinities, and move away. "It has been hard waiting so long.... Now go." The young man leaves hurriedly. The wardens come to fetch the prisoner: he is dead.

"They went back over the dossier of the case, the interrogations, et cetera. This sham bandit knew Sanskrit.

" 'Why were you found with the others?'

" 'I was traveling toward the town with them. They said to me: "Stay with us, We need you." I stayed.'

" 'Why?'

" 'What did it matter?'

"Nothing had been of any importance until it was a question of keeping death waiting: he was waiting for the young visitor in order to die."

Again that haunting "What does it matter?" At the time of that conversation, I had no experience of the approach of the unknown. Today I am struck not so much by the story as by my friend's familiarity with psychic states akin to the one I have just experienced—by his domestication of death, which is something that India may owe to metempsychosis.

It is five o'clock before my lucidity succumbs to the fever.

Part
III

Any sensation that one has just discovered pervades the memory. My strange vertigo obsesses me. Real vertigo is something I have never experienced. The phrase *to lose one's foothold on life* keeps running through my head, linked to the image of an aircraft sideslipping in an air pocket. I was heavily clamped to a magnetic floor; I remembered the astronauts floating in their cabin and donning space suits with weighted boots in order to walk on the moon. The consciousness of being alive enveloped me like a space suit, ready to abandon me in the inexplicable weightlessness of the void; death is no doubt what follows.

It happens that I have suddenly discovered life, after having escaped death; I shall never forget the clothespins bobbing on their wire like swallows on the first morning after the tank trap. Now I have experienced this feeling turned inside out: I suddenly discovered something other than nonhuman life. I did not take it for death; but it speaks of death.

After the event, I encountered the god of dread. Dread independent of fear, like sexuality independent of any object (except ourselves). Fear of what? Of death? Not so. No connection with the prickling of every hair on my body during the seconds that followed being dragged from the shattered aircraft. Fear, even when retrospective, is fear of something. My feeling was to anxiety what terror is to fright. Far beyond fear. Deep inside me, as much a part of me as the beating of my heart. A sacred horror inhabits us, awaits us, as the mystics tell us that God awaits them.

Death sucks us in. I am still haunted by the funnel of sand at the bottom of which a murderous insect lies in wait for the ants. I remember an illustrated edition of Edgar Allan Poe in which there was a picture of a tiny boat caught in the irresistible funnel of the maelstrom. But I am not the boat. No religion, no experience has taught us that dread is *within us*. The fact of having experienced it imperceptibly separates me from it. The inner forces which drive us to self-destruction, to shame, provoke despair rather than terror; this force does not drive us to anything. I encountered it in the way that a psychiatrist discovers within himself the spiders and octopuses of his patients' nightmares. The monster occupied my ruins, then my consciousness, which was sinking into sleep; finally the path melted away—but I had recognized it, and I shall recognize it again, like one of those dreams in which one thinks: I have already dreamt that.

A heap of iron filings stuck to the magnet of the earth, but also a struggling prisoner (although I was certainly not moving), kinsman of the soldiers of the Vistula in their heartrending spasm of revulsion. The fear-induced images played their dreamlike game, between the convulsions of the Russians—their shadowy forms like shot rabbits in the decomposed forest—and the blurred, twitching figures in the photographs of Hiroshima. The haunting power of that event is akin to that of myth. Challenging death—and, in a more obscure way, the dead, for those German soldiers were acting against the will of their fellow Germans killed in that war—belongs to the realm of myth. A myth whose hero is neither a nation nor a people, but man; because the Germans in the trench and the Frenchmen in the camp merged in my mind into the voices of the cavemen of prehistory, and man alone, mute babbler, is the protagonist of the archaic myth.

I remembered (still the same word, *convulsion?*) a gallows in the extermination camp which we liberated. The condemned men, hands tied, ropes round their necks, were supporting their weight by their big toes, suspended between weakness and torture. We thought at first that they were already hanged, and were about to march on, when they yelled after us.

I am haunted by the struggle against the poison gas, not by the gallows. Is this because I pinned down the events of the Vistula long ago, or because, amid the unfortunates surrounding me here, that crazed, bloodless struggle may seem a premonition? The gas is the Scourge—the harbinger of death.

As the days pass, the stupefying experience gradually fades and transforms itself into a blurred cataclysm. The threat is still present, or would be were it not for the murmur of the hospital; lucidity, always intermittent, sometimes becomes more acute.

A daydream follows its desultory course, even when it deems itself a consecutive train of thought. Hemlock brings back suicide, Socrates, and the account of his last hours. I discovered the clue to its tone when reading the Crucifixion according to St. John. Speaking in the language of the Panathenaea, Socrates, despite his tedious theory of the soul, has the chance to disregard pain until his final words: "Crito, I owe a cock to Asclepius; do not forget to pay it...." To whom could he address his offering from Hades with a more friendly complicity than to the god who had cured him of life?

Set against this end, the agony of Christ. "And he went forth bearing his cross into a place called the place of a skull, which is called in the Hebrew Golgotha." Jesus will say only: "Woman, behold thy son," "I thirst," and then, "It is finished." And, according to St. Mark, "Lama sabachthani."

From this account of the Passion, akin to the darkness that covers the earth when Christ expires, the sculptors of the Rhineland, Grünewald, and the Spaniards have extracted images which evoke the charnel house. The Crucifixion is more profound than this eloquence. No one speaks with serenity under torture. Socrates, who converses nobly with Death, would have nothing to say to Torture. The pencil broke on Valéry's last sentence: "After all, no one before Christianity had said that God is love." No one, since the existence of speech, has answered the slave woman born in vain who offered to the gods of Rome her child who had died in vain.

My Vercors chaplain knew only what he had learned from the seminary in Lyon (he had never been to Paris) and from his own unquenchable charity of heart. It was he who had baptized the Jews hand over fist because "some of it might stick." He was dumbfounded by the story of the Vistula offensive. When I sent him *The Brothers Karamazov*, telling him how struck many of us had been by Ivan's remark "If the world permits the torture of an innocent child by a brute, I don't repudiate God, but I'm handing in my ticket," he had written to me: "It's a terrible problem, because it's the problem of Evil. . . . But Evil isn't stronger than Redemption, Redemption is stronger than Evil." Myself, though I do not believe in Redemption, I have come to the conclusion that the enigma of cruelty is no more tantalizing than that of the simplest act of heroism or love. But sacrifice alone can look torture in the face, and the God of Christianity would not be God without the Crucifixion.

A new patient is brought into the next-door room. He, perhaps, will not die. What did my poor neighbor think? My comrades in Spain and France used to say "Too bad," with a fleeting thought for those they loved. They had fulfilled the caste duty of volunteers, which confers knighthood on anyone who dies for what he has chosen. My father? Did he think what I am thinking today? Almost all the people I have loved were killed in accidents. And yet Josette, who knew I would come from the battlefront and who had asked for her beautiful face to be made up before my arrival, said the same thing as the wisest of my friends, Bernard Groethuysen, who was riddled with cancer: "I'd never have thought dying would be like this."

Taboo forbids me to imagine myself cured, and I forbid myself to feel I am doomed. My family is ingrained in me, but I only visit the cemetery out of a sense of duty. I remember All Souls' Day in Mexico, banquets among the tombs, the distribution of sugar skeletons to the children, the basket makers working overtime to produce their death's-head straw mermaids before nightfall. I remember the murmuring of the Indians in the church in Guatemala, kneeling in front of rows of candles that spoke to them of their dead children, the buzz of tender, funereal chatter accompanying the flames down toward the flower-strewn floor. China, land of ancestor-worship, has banished death. When I met Clappique again in Singapore, the Papuans banged their gongs and drums to hail the white steamers laden with all the ghosts of Oceania, where the ghosts are whiter than Europeans. Theaters of truth, like corridas. Nothing else. The sense of survival after death is unknown to me.

Multiple footsteps in the corridor. The head of the neurology department?

No. It is my professor friend, the one who came to see me on the first day to say that nothing was irreversible. With his tall, gangling silhouette, still reminiscent of a jovial General de Gaulle, he enters the room alone, waving his arms in the air, but the smallness of the room or the atmosphere of the clinic (to which he is nevertheless accustomed, since he is the head of one of the principal psychiatric units in Paris) contrasts his gaiety with the austerity of the besmocked consultants.

I offer him cigarettes.

"Thanks, I prefer English ones. I wonder why it is that I like English tobacco, tea, whiskey, breakfast, marmalade, when I don't care a damn about England. I suppose it all goes together, like our own cuisine, wine, painting, female fashions."

True enough, I have always seen him dressed in the traditional English style of his youth, tweeds and crepe soles; like the foreign service, the medical profession has changed style, and replaced the traditional black jackets with tweeds. He has just been interrogating his neurologist colleagues, and brings me nothing but good news, though the danger is still present. Anecdotes follow, either because he wants to take my mind off my illness or to test me. Before my arrival here, he said to me: "We're now ahead of the United States. If Hemingway had been treated in Switzerland or France instead of going to the Mayo Clinic, he wouldn't have killed himself." I ask him about his own work, which is endless, like that of all psychiatrists. "This week, I've had the usual good results, although nobody has any idea what makes these damned drugs work. However, it's better to cure people without knowing why than let them die while knowing how! I've had one unfortunate case. I suspected that the girl would put one over on me someday or other, but when they called me she was already dead. I'd treated her some time ago: fantasist, perverse, very intelligent. The mother came to consult me with a tape recorder: it was a monologue in which the daughter confided to an imaginary friend—probably herself—her reasons for committing suicide. Then the revolver shot. She certainly didn't miss! She'd already tried. They nearly all try again. Not immediately. They leave you in peace for a few months. They're obstinate, you know, but so is life."

"How do you define life, in your field?"

I am lying down, and he has remained standing. Seen from below, his rather naïve looks (although his perspicacity is well-known), with the fair hair flopping over a prematurely bald patch, take on a stern expression. But he laughs:

"Definitions of life, indeed yes, I have several of those!"

Men's laughter often reveals their childhood faces. The professor becomes simultaneously a humorous patrician and a curly-headed urchin, despite his bald patch; then he becomes serious again:

"Life? I know about it because I'm always running after it—in other words, I know very little—like most people. Here, it's coma alternating with lucidity.... We see far fewer deaths than we used to, you know. People die at home. When I was an intern, we performed two autopsies a day. Whereas during the whole of this year the hospital has done only three. Three! They were fascinating, autopsies: a way of proving that one's diagnosis was right...."

He closes his eyes.

"But pain can alter a lot of things. It's another matter altogether...."

"What helps the seriously ill?"

"Christians, you know, die in accordance with what they believe about divine judgment or divine mercy; they seldom know in advance. There are surprises. As there are with others.... Except, almost always, with skeptics."

"They face up to it better?"

The childish look fades from his features. He answers slowly, weighing his words:

"They almost never face up to it, did you know that? Never. The 'soft pillow of doubt' is worse than acute depression, and worse than cancer.... Your poor neighbor had a very bad time, they tell me."

"Was he young or old?"

"Sixtyish.... An intellectual."

All I knew of my poor white mouse were the muffled screams—and his anxiety. He had cried, "Don't hurt me!"

"Science," my friend goes on, "has made far fewer atheists than skeptics, you know. In the last analysis, the Anatole France attitude is fairly widespread. The motto is 'What does it matter!' For us doctors, a real sense of futility used to be a grave symptom."

"Lawrence of Arabia had it inscribed on the wall of his cottage."

"Well, it's the first thing a suicide mutters to us. It has nothing to do with the airy questioning of a Montaigne, who in any case believed in God. You can be skeptical about a great many things, but not about a corpse. And not here. You can pretend to in books...."

He is even taller than Jacques Méry, and his semaphore gesticulations on arrival reminded me, by contrast, of the chilly gestures of my Singapore friend. It was Jacques Méry who told me about Lawrence's inscription.

"You know, we treat it now, futility. And it..."

"Would you have cured Lawrence?"

"Who knows? I'm treating you, after all! But would he have agreed to treatment? What I wanted to say was that patients cured of acute depression sometimes go to the opposite extreme—I don't know what to call it, the disease of cocksureness. I remember a parishioner I once treated for a neurosis verging on the suicidal. She had been unfaithful to her husband while he was a prisoner of war. She was utterly ravaged with guilt. Having been cured by amphetamines, she disappeared, then turned up again after a few months and said to me, 'I really wonder why I attached so much importance to it all!' 'Perhaps you had reason to, madame, since you told me you could never forgive yourself for having been unfaithful to your husband; especially as he was a prisoner at the time, and you're deeply religious....'"

He rubs his hands in a canonical manner, and then raises one of them, which seems to unfurl above his head as he mimics the indignation of his lady patient:

" 'Doctor, if he hadn't been a prisoner I should probably have had no occasion to be unfaithful to him. As for my religious sentiments, if God doesn't understand me, who else will?'

"You see, humanity reminds me of that good lady. Me too, sometimes.... One century is obsessed by its depressive or paranoid neuroses, the next one wonders why they attached so much importance to all that...."

In Barcelona, toward the end of the Spanish civil war, I was reading a history of social doctrines when the dismal, sinister wail of the sirens filled the town, which was instantaneously plunged into darkness. I went on reading by the light of a pocket torch hidden under the sheets. The book, which predated Lenin, knew nothing of the technique of insurrection and, true to its title, defined every revolutionary notion in terms of a doctrine—as though it were a study of the history of utopias, of all the ideal societies that had ever been dreamed up, from Thomas More to the anarchists, from Fourier to Kropotkin. This immense aberration trembled at the approach of the enemy bombers. Of the passions it had once inspired, nothing remained. The latest drives out all the rest. The demon which the Far East calls the demon of "things-that-pass" spoke to me not in the polite tones of social theory but with the deep roar of blood. "What does it matter!"—but the prisoner still persevered with his escape attempts. Those things that pass, those dreams, had been hailed like the dawn whose dull pink glow was beginning to suffuse the ceiling of my room to the accompaniment of the first arpeggio of bombs. But it was not the dawn. I had chosen the top floor of the hotel, which was always free in those days, and I got up to watch the fires which lit up the window. From it the nocturnal city could be seen stretching as far as the hills. The insidious softness of the red glow and the tranquil plumes of smoke followed in the wake of the explosions, and the gigantic flourish formed by the smoke trails spread slowly across the sky like the long train of utopias and revolts. The bombs and the anti-aircraft guns stopped simultaneously, the all-clear siren and a squealing of children filled the glowing silence, and I thought of the poor of Madrid, laden with their scarlet quilts and sewing machines, when the pawn shops were ordered to hand them back their pledges.

I recount all this to the professor, who remarks:

"It's a faculty of our funny old brain, you know. . . . But when it becomes obsessive, watch out! When he had his inscription carved, Lawrence of Arabia was giving notice of his death. One can always find a motorcycle to kill oneself with. Do you often recall that night in Barcelona, here?"

"Often? No."

"Thank God for that! What form does the memory take?"

"It starts with the procession of utopian hopes and expectations, I think; and I hear the creaking of someone's new shoes in the silence that falls just before the all clear."

He makes a vague gesture which seems to mean: let's go back a bit.

"You once wrote that Death with a capital *D*, your metaphysical Death . . ."

"Shiva."

". . . Shiva, if you like, is not at all identical with decease. It was from that point on that I began to read you attentively. You gave the answer in terms of art."

"What I chiefly said was that art was unintelligible if one ignored the problem you speak of. . . ."

(One of the characters in *The Walnut Trees of Altenburg* says something like: "The greatest mystery is not that we should have been flung at random amid the profusion of life and of the stars, but that in what Pascal calls our prison we can draw from ourselves images powerful enough to deny our nothingness. . . .")

"All right, yes, if you like," the professor goes on. "But all the same, you were thinking of war. I've come across the same experience in hospital. But now that resuscitation has become an integral part of medicine. . . . Ultimately, resuscitation, deep-freezing, and such don't eliminate the metaphysical question posed by death, since it concerns the meaning of life. But still, the 'last hours' are slipping through our fingers."

"Have you noticed that women, even when they're believers, attach less importance to their last hours than men do?"

"Listen, men and Christianity, all right, I'll grant you that, but also antiquity. Do you know what happened to the codirector of this clinic, Lhermitte? There was a girl in a coma, at the Necker: no response from the nervous system, heart, respiration; circulation kept going by resuscitation. Called in as a consultant, he examined her thoroughly and was flummoxed. He examined her again and finally said, 'I believe this patient has been dead for three days.' And the autopsy proved him right. The brain had dissolved. I sometimes feel I ought to deep-freeze my patients for a hundred years, and when they returned to life, medicine would have made the advances necessary to cure them. A weird idea. Not knowing when patients die complicates death for us; but ultimately, searching for the 'when' distracts us from searching for the 'why.'"

He is no more concerned than I am about being right. What impresses me about him is the human experience suggested by his words: "They don't try again immediately; they leave you in peace for a few months...." "I struggle on, in the end not very successfully, like the rest of humanity...." "Skeptics almost never face up to it...." "My parishioner..." "Our funny old brain..." "They were fascinating, autopsies...." "I ought to deep-freeze my patients...." This intelligent man comprehends what obsesses me here, through a corpus of knowledge and research which is almost beyond my ken. If the human species is less unique for him than for me, that is because I think of what is particular about it whereas he thinks of what is general. What is to me a threat is for him part of a day's work.

"What do resuscitated patients themselves think about it?" I ask him.

"The suicides?" (There are others!) "They're euphoric. Not because they've recovered a taste for life. Just like that. There are some who *have been* dead, you know. No memory of it. The mystery continues. The others, the 'intensive care' patients, think nothing. Unless they're in pain; then they think of the pain. Those who suffer very little pain are more numerous than you might think, especially here. People find it difficult to think about something they're unfamiliar with. They're not used to being in a coma, you know!"

"In the great ages of faith people thought of death as something familiar...."

"But everyone knew quite well that the experience of death can't be repeated! In the last resort my atheist colleagues believe in extinction and my Christian colleagues in salvation—in the same way: it's six of one and half a dozen of the other. To believe that biology will eventually explain life and the human species is no more improbable than the opposite. The ultimate knowledge is perhaps a sublime carrot: we go on running after it without ever reaching it, of course, but the limits of mathematics don't send us back to the abacus! We can always get one stage further—and after that we die ..."

"Or before...."

"... and it's up to the next generation. Man invents a lot of things; in fact he has just invented molecular biology.... You know, we've learned more about the chemistry of the brain in the last fifteen years than had been learned in the previous five thousand."

What is one to make of the intellectual dispassion that goes so well with his smile? But it isn't the latest discoveries that actuate him, it is the object of the research he conducts so passionately, and puts before everything else.

"In my prisoner-of-war camp," I observe, "a priest told me that a lot of people die in an inextricable mixture of fear and hope. But he also told me that a dying man had thrown him out so as to be able to finish *The Mysteries of Paris.*"

"And anyhow, what does it mean, thinking about death? Is anxiety a thought?"

"In a sense, yes. . . ."

Thoughts about death are always more or less fruitless, like those of Socrates when he seeks to demonstrate the existence of the soul. Agreed. And yet the feeling, the awareness of death exists: a feeling without an object, like anxiety, one that invents its object. The semi-openmindedness which my illness often permits me has shown me the extent to which pain nurtures that feeling: if I suffered more I should be far more tyrannized by death. Christianity seems to be highly complacent on this subject—especially from the fifteenth century onward. I once did some research into the origin of the Pietà as a subject. Without success.

Meditation on death after the age of fifty, long practiced in the Christian world, contributed not a little toward nurturing its deadly virus. The Indian sage had a tryst with death, and went out to meet it in the forest and become united with the absolute. Whereas many of our dueling maniacs, survivors of a score of fights, ended up overcome with religious masochism: "These feet that ran so swiftly, these hands that opened to give, will move no more; these eyes will see no more. . . ." Christianity has poked around assiduously among the embers of death to find the presence of God—which it has often forgotten in pursuit of its meticulous evocation of suffering.

"Do you know, when I cure one of my parishioners, or when I stave off pain or insanity, in the end what you call the 'absurd' takes a beating. All that will last a few generations, eh? But why should it last, in the end? You put it very well when you wrote: 'What is the point of going to the moon, if it's only to commit suicide there?' Do I believe in the conclusions of biology? I believe in them more than in anything else. They answer less inadequately the questions death poses."

"It always seems as if its answers must be an *explanation* of the world and of man; as if it were saying: genetics explains well what Genesis explained badly. But you can see that even that explanation has its shadowy areas. The origin of the 'primordial soup' from which life emerges. Then, the emergence itself. And then man's arrival on the scene. A link in the evolutionary chain? If so, certainly not the same sort of link as all the others. In spite of the affinities. And this difference interests me—challenges me?— as much as the evolution of species."

"Isn't there as much difference between a village idiot and ... you, for instance, as between an ape and the said idiot?"

"The species to which the village idiot and I belong has certain basic aptitudes—self-questioning, for instance—that no ape has ever possessed.... Incidentally, you study this question in terms of species, and yet there you are, talking about individuals; whereas I who take the individual as my starting point am now talking in terms of species. Curious, isn't it? And there's something else that intrigues me even more: this conversation demands careful attention, and yet I'm not tired."

"The Pertofrane added to your medication this morning is a stimulant."

"Right, then, let's go on. What we're discussing, aren't we, is the way you try to make sense of the adventure of life, in somewhat the same way as history has turned the human adventure into a destiny."

The memory of that night in Singapore with Méry was still in my mind:

"I once heard the question posed 'at the source.' In Asia, one of my friends said to me: 'When I'm in the tropical forest I can't help thinking: men were faced with all this, and they knew nothing. The biologists tell us that countless selections and a hereditary, accumulated experience, an experience of the species, enabled them to eat only what they *should* eat in order to survive. If they had had to experiment, as we more or less believe, there would have been no accumulation of experience; humanity would have disappeared, poisoned.' "

"The experiments went on for a very long time. . . ."

" 'The jungle cries out to us that man hadn't a chance,' my friend went on. 'Another force operated. A force that crops up in many other spheres, like electricity when its discovery was in the offing. . . . The bird that lives on the pulp of the strychnos, the tree strychnine comes from, never touches the kernel, a fatal poison. . . .' "

"Birds never eat kernels as a rule."

He laughs. Jacques Méry's features changed too when he

laughed. Like him, the professor seems to have acquired his face by accident. Méry ended up by softening and saddening his centurion's mask; the professor had ended up by deliberately subduing his jovially nonchalant gestures, his wide-eyed expression. His features have their work cut out matching up with his personality. The result is not without charm, and his success with women is well-known. Were it not for his hardheaded remarks, he would remind me of a familiar stereotype from Hollywood films: the shy, gangling, awkward fellow who charms all the girls and always wins in the end.

"Perhaps the kernels are sometimes open," I remark. "The fact is often cited, as you know; stories about curare and belladonna are very popular. Let's take another example."

"Yes, indeed, I can think of lots!"

"Then I'll spare you mine. Anyway, I'm inclined to think, like my friend, that some of the instincts of animals, their migrations for instance, are not the result of selection. Although the migrations are 'programmed,' to use the fashionable term. Moreover, my friend pointed out, the canine species hasn't transmitted to any breed of dog the instinctive rejection of poisoned tidbits. He quoted the phrase of your colleague Haldane in this context: 'If it's God, why not say so!'"

"Was he a believer?"

"No, agnostic, with a tinge of Buddhism."

"So he didn't offer any solution? Well, a plausible explanation is better than none at all."

"Plausible, provided you leave man out. Species... It

isn't the ant species, or for that matter the lion species, who possess an inexhaustible proclivity for conceiving other worlds, for calling our world into question; it's mankind, who has created (almost by the way!) speech, writing, tools, the tomb, and other gadgets—as well as the means of blowing up the planet. Does one have to be a Christian, then, to think that man is separated from all the rest by a difference in kind, not degree? Somehow or other he's beginning to get accustomed to the unthinkable. And when Pascal speaks of man he isn't always wrong, even without the soul, even without God. It isn't some exploit or other in the Andes that no animal would have been capable of, it's the Beyond. Please don't imagine that I'm in pursuit of an immortal soul. You know the story of the Martian who spent a few hours on earth and didn't come across any men, but found a Kodak camera. He takes it away in his flying saucer and discovers how it works. This contraption is so manifestly *organized* to take pictures that it must be a living creature. Quite right—if one doesn't know about Kodak. We grope, we get warmer, and eventually we find Kodak. After which we discover that understanding Kodak is much more difficult than understanding the camera. I don't in the least expect to find the key to the universe— simply a further clue. What for? Well, to go on running, as you put it. Perhaps also because I'd like to know what becomes of man, without God—and here."

He seems about to reply, but then stops. My "here" embarrasses him. I go on:

"This seems to me the essential point, whichever way we

interpret instincts and human nature. The interpretations
of the universe, of mankind, which preceded science were
the religions, weren't they? Well, every great religion
revealed the world simultaneously in terms of an explanation—myth, history, et cetera—and of a meaning. With
evolution, for the first time—I repeat, for the first time—we
have an explanation of the world that doesn't offer a
meaning. There was, not for very long, the struggle for
life. . . ."

"Which doesn't come from Darwin."

"I know—from Spencer. In any case, outdated in your
eyes. But a point I'd like to make is that the Bible wasn't
primarily a story, from which the Christian drew conclusions later. The narrative was inseparable from its meaning,
secreted its own values. Men found their Law in it, in the
widest sense of the word: they didn't look for it there.
They don't find it in either the primordial soup or
evolution."

"Yes indeed. But will they find it again in the Bible?"

"They wanted to live according to Christ or Buddha.
How could they possibly live according to Darwin,
Mendel, or whomever? Any more than Einstein, Newton,
or Planck."

"Why shouldn't Einstein be the successor to St. Paul?"

"The Christian, through the medium of St. Paul,
partakes of Christ; the average man doesn't partake of
relativity, or the universe, through Einstein. He respects
him. He envies him, perhaps. But science changes the earth,
it doesn't change man. Christ, Buddha, Mohammed

addressed themselves to him. Science doesn't. Since men ceased to expect happiness from it, they're afraid of it."

"It would be extremely interesting to compare what science meant to people before 1914 and what's become of it since."

"Scientism was a bombastic little god, not very durable; science is becoming an omnipotent god, half clandestine, and the arbiter of civilization throughout the world, whether it likes it or not. All science posits truth as the supreme value, but that truth is a supreme value only for scientists themselves. People have made light of the remark of Dostoevsky's character: 'If I were forced to choose between Christ and truth, I should take Christ's side against truth.' Those people are wrong. The new god can do more than all the others, since it can destroy the planet. But it's a silent god."

"Interesting. . . . According to you, I suppose that would explain the youth crisis?"

"What is beginning to disappear is the molding, the fashioning of man. Science can destroy the planet, but it can't fashion a man. The humane sciences illustrate this to perfection. Man is not what they posit, but what they seek. What used to explain the world was what had molded men—in molding itself, so to speak. Not only religions: the Roman who dazzled Europe from the Renaissance to Napoleon wasn't a religious type."

"Why shouldn't they learn to mold themselves?"

"Western man remains half-formed because he's waiting. Science *qua* belief and not *qua* knowledge is belief in a *future* explanation of the world. And Westerners always give the impression of believing they're going to supersede the Crusades with a world-wide campaign of civic instruction. Modern man has been fashioned on the basis of exemplary stereotypes: saint, chevalier, caballero, gentleman, bolshevik, and so on. The exemplariness belongs to the realm of fancy, of fiction. And the fiction of science—no pun intended—is science fiction."

"Even if one accepts your analysis, why shouldn't man succeed in molding himself?" He speaks almost in an undertone, as though communing with himself. Then he finds his voice again:

"It's less difficult than inventing fire.... You're right on one point: he's going through a sort of no-man's-land. He's beginning to realize it, you know. For a century or so he'll try and get through it by postponing everything that can be postponed. Suspending judgment is not as silly as skepticism.... It will be a rough passage...."

He sits down. This must mean that he thinks my lucidity is going to last a little longer. His resemblance to General de Gaulle fades. His nose is ever so slightly turned up, his mouth small and round. He clasps his hands round one of his knees. His voice has sunk with him; not exactly graver, but more abstracted, like the voice of our obsessions and our daydreams:

"What I'm going to say may surprise you. Both personally and as a doctor, I think doubt is always superficial. And, moreover, very bad. It's always accompanied with smug, knowing smiles. Idiotic, because everything it brings with it feeds anxiety: uncertainty, skepticism, procrastination. Faced with the physical fact of death, the corpse, it doesn't measure up. Death wins for some reason that isn't clear, but which is a reason nonetheless."

"The corpse weighed little in the presence of the gods. Now it's become burdensome."

"And do you know what it becomes when it responds to skepticism? It's very surprising: a kind of taunt."

"Only religions knew how to respond to death. No doubt that's what they were invented for. . . ."

Prince Siddhartha, coming across a cremation in the warm Indian night, is told: "Prince, that is what is called a dead man." For centuries painters and hermits contemplated the famous death's-head grin. But the professor is right: skulls have never laughed so much as they do at us.

"The power of the corpse lies in the realization that *I* will be *this.*" He points a finger at his chest, then at the ground, seems to look to me to bear him out, his expression wide-eyed, almost ingenuous. Then he goes on:

"But for each one of us, 'this' means other people's corpses. No one has ever seen his own corpse, you know."

"The Greeks proclaimed it long ago: the living cannot conceive death or feel it—and neither can the dead."

"They proclaimed it; but in the last resort no one has ever put it to the test. Our relationship with death is tied up with a system of belief, true enough, but after years of seeing people die I sometimes wonder if, for the unconscious mind, the content of that belief isn't the transmigration of man into the dead body. Just think of it. Metempsychosis dies devilish hard; in Asia and elsewhere it's still a powerful force. The corpse fosters anxiety among men who don't believe in a Last Judgment: we suffer from an anxiety of the beyond, not of the here and now. Our death doesn't pose the same questions as the birth of our grandfather! I spend my time treating anxiety; it feeds on death, death doesn't create it."

He smiles now as if to suggest that this conversation is not to be taken seriously. I feel inclined to think, not talk. In any case, he gets up.

"I have another patient here, who's coming out tomorrow, I hope. She's a relation of Georges Pompidou. Ah, well, for a man in your condition you're not doing too badly! Keep those bees buzzing in your bonnet!"

In the old days professors used to be more solemn—but then in those days they were always older than I.... He goes off, leaving the door open, and, once in the corridor, resumes the movements that swing his briefcase along.

Rest. Or stagnation. Except that ... How shall I define what I felt that night in Barcelona, what struck me again so forcibly as I looked out at the streets on the way to the Salpêtrière, and which has no name in the West—the sense of the "passing-of-things," as the Buddhists say? I think from time to time, In the year 1973 before the Christian Era, in the Egyptian Middle Kingdom ... Today I think, What did they say about death in 1573? I know a little about what was written, but what was said? ... Fatigue is setting in. During my talk with the professor I felt recovered; now I am sinking back into unconsciousness as though into sleep. Lulled by fleeting fragments of poems without beginning or end, lines from Shakespeare: "In such a night as this,/When the sweet wind did gently kiss the trees..." "In such a night/Medea gather'd the enchanted herbs...."; serenity of so many poems about death; Piero della Francesca, the Avignon Pietà, Monteverdi's vespers, the *Crucifixerunt* of Bach; love, when fate has not obliterated it...

Fraternity, which fate does not obliterate.

Why is it the faithful companion of death? I feel the need of it today, doubtless in response to my memory of Barcelona; the drugs, even in this somnolent state, help to guide my memories. And under the influence of the new medication, my somnolence is accompanied by an intoxicating flow of images, as, earlier, of ideas. Fraternity is rarely absent from these images, and the scenes on the Vistula haunted me because of it. People think they understand fraternity because they confuse it with human warmth; in fact it is a sentiment that comes from the depths, added almost as an afterthought to the motto of the Republic, whose first flags bore only the words *Liberty, Equality*.

Liberty, Equality! Every revolt loses many of its initial sentiments, and even many of those that preceded it: scientism made fanatical attempts to conceive of religions divorced from the sacred; sincere and intelligent Russians lauded liberty at the same time as the Ogpu.* But at least the word *liberty* has retained its prestige, whereas *fraternity* now merely suggests a comical utopia in which no one is

---

* The Soviet secret police, later NKVD, now KGB. (Tr.)

nasty to anyone else. Men believe that fraternity was added on as a makeweight to more profound sentiments like justice or freedom. But it is not just a superficial appendage. Like the sacred, it eludes us if we strip it of its primitive, irrational element. As mysterious as love, and as divorced from right-mindedness or duty; like love—and unlike liberty—a provisional sentiment, a state of grace. If the Feast of the Federation on July 14 convulsed France, it was because it was the Feast of Fraternity. Let us guard against giving it its trivialized name, and its true essence will reverberate with the same profound resonance as love, sacrifice, the supernatural, and death. "Men will one day learn to live according to the dictates of the heart...." A combatant in the Spanish civil war once said to me: "The opposite of humiliation and death is not liberty, as they tell us, but fraternity." Of the words of the Republican motto, this forgotten word is the only one that echoes Christianity; my Spaniard would have considered that the Crucifixion, too, meant fraternity.

I have spoken of love. A memory of 1925 or thereabouts. Like most young idiots at the time, I did not believe in its existence. In a little cinema, when the lights went on again, I saw Nénette and Rintintin in the flesh, both eighteen years old.* They were not even kissing each other. They were gazing into each other's eyes. With such rapt wonderment that I was reminded of those insects one can

---

* Nénette and Rintintin were the names given in France to little mascot dolls popular in the twenties. (Tr.)

kill without being able to sever their embrace. Clinging to one another as the dying cling to the red-hot iron of their agony.

True fraternity. In the Panthéon, I felt the warmth "which penetrated the bitter cold," in the words of one of the surviving relations of Jean Moulin:

"In a village in the Corrèze, the Germans had killed some maquisards, and ordered the mayor to have them buried secretly at dawn. It is the custom for the women of the neighborhood to attend the funeral of any villager by standing beside the grave of their own family. No one knew these dead men, since they were Alsatians. When they reached the cemetery, borne by our peasants under the menacing submachine guns of a German guard, the ebbing tide of darkness revealed the black-clad village women motionless upon the hillside, each by her family grave, silently awaiting the burial of the French dead."

These images pursue one another as the illuminated message heralding the war superseded the advertisements in the square in Montpellier; images of the only sentiment which, until the fever returns, will dare to contemplate death.

At Roquebrune, in front of the log fire, the moment when the man of forty is gripped for the first time by the disease of remembrance. Remembrance of what? Of that day in Saigon, at the time we were publishing *L'Indochine enchaînée*. No printer would dare take on the typesetting.

Our workers had reassembled some old presses. We had only been able to find (at the mission in Hong Kong) some English type, without accents. Impossible to print the paper. That night an Annamese worker came in and pulled out of his pocket a knotted handkerchief, its corners standing up like rabbits' ears: "There's nothing but *e*'s. Acute accents, grave accents, circumflexes. Diaereses, more difficult. P'raps they can do without them. Tomorrow, Annamese bring some more." He opened the handkerchief, emptied a jumble of characters onto a press-stone, and aligned them with an expert finger, without another word. He had taken them from the government printing works, and knew that if he was betrayed he would be sent to prison not as a revolutionary but as a thief.

The most striking instance of fraternity I know, one that I thought up myself... In a hotel in Peïra-Cava, I was writing the scene in *Man's Fate* in which the wounded Shanghai revolutionaries are about to be flung into the furnace of the locomotive. Katow has managed to hang on to his cyanide. During the night, his hand touches the hand of Kyo, who has been thrown in beside him and who grasps it. At that moment I realized that Katow was going to place the cyanide in the hand that had just clasped his.

During the Resistance, I had some cyanide in my possession for almost two years. When it was sent to us from London, I wondered whether the scene in my book would turn out to have been prophetic. As prophetic as the story of the Vistula amid the convulsions of my poor comrades? In part—for I would not, alas, have given my cyanide away.

Another scene, which I transposed in *The Days of Wrath*.
Boris Savinkov in prison, with the other condemned men who are about to be hanged. When his name is called out, another prisoner steps forward. The terrorists know that Savinkov is one of the leaders of the movement, that his life must be saved, and they look at one another with pride. All except him.

Scenes of Spain that I have written, filmed, or wanted to film. Others that I had forgotten.
The military hospital in Madrid, like a vaulted cellar out of Goya, dim light filtering through the plants covering the skylight. Under the veil of his mosquito net, a wounded man screams. An airman, shot down with his bombs, twenty-seven fragments. A woman—his mother?—thrusts her head under the mosquito net. The screams subside. Soon I can no longer even hear the grinding of teeth that followed them. From inside, a hand can be seen twisting the mosquito net. A new sound begins, grows more distinct: a sound made by lips. What use are words in the presence of a lacerated body? The mother is doing the only thing she can: she is kissing it.

The sermon of the monk from Los Hurdes to the militiamen in the darkness filled with the roar of army lorries.

"Christ Jesus thought things weren't right in our country. He said to himself, I'll go there. The angel looked around for the best woman in the region. Jesus was about to appear to her when she said, 'Oh, don't bother: the child would come before its time, seeing I wouldn't have enough to eat.'

"So Christ went to another woman. There was nothing but rats around the cradle. A bit small for keeping the baby warm, and not much in the way of company. So Jesus thought to himself that things were as bad as ever in Spain.

"The landowners were made to give some land to the peasants. The ones who had oxen screamed that they were being plundered. By those who had rats. And they called in the Roman soldiers.

"So then the Lord went to Madrid. And to shut his mouth the kings of the world began to slaughter the children of Madrid.

"Then Christ said to himself that there really wasn't much to be done with men. They were so foul that even if you bled for them night and day for all eternity you'd never manage to wash them clean.

"The descendants of the Three Kings hadn't come to his second birth, seeing as they'd become tramps or government officials. Then, for the first time in the history of the world, the very first, from every country, those that were quite near and those that were thousands of miles away, those where it was hot and those where it was freezing cold, everybody who was brave and poor set off *with their guns.*

"And they knew in their hearts that Christ Jesus was

alive among the poor of our country. And in long processions, from every country, those who knew enough about poverty to fight against it, with their guns if they had any and their hands if they hadn't, one after another they came to sleep on the soil of Spain.

"They spoke every language, and there were even Chinese shoelace-peddlers among them.

"And when everyone had done enough killing—and when the last file of the poor had set out on the march . . ."

The final words in a hushed voice, with the whispered intensity of a sorcerer's incantation:

". . . a star that no one had ever seen rose above them."

The return of the wounded from the bomber shot down in the sierras of Teruel, the stretchers carried by peasants and followed by the people of all the villages through which the procession passed.

The little township is massed behind its crenellated walls. The light is dim, but night has not yet fallen. Although there has been no rain, the pavestones are shiny, and the stretcher bearers pick their way carefully. In the houses whose upper stories project above the ramparts, a few dim lights are glimmering.

The peasants standing on the ramparts are solemn but unshocked. The face of the first casualty is above the blanket, and it is intact. The atmosphere grows more somber when his successors pass: there is still enough light for watchful eyes to see the large bloodstains on the leather.

When Gardet arrives, a hush so profound descends on this already silent crowd that the muffled roar of distant torrents is suddenly audible.

All the other wounded men can see; and all, even the bombardier, have made an effort to smile on seeing the crowd. Gardet does not look at them. He is alive: from the ramparts, the coffin can be seen behind him. Blind, then? Covered by a blanket up to his chin, with the bandage under his flying-helmet lying so flat that there cannot be any nose beneath it, this wounded man is the incarnation of warfare as peasants such as these have immemorially conceived of it. And he is a volunteer. For a moment they hesitate, not knowing what to do; then resolutely, like those of the other villages, they raise their clenched fists in silence.

It has begun to drizzle. The last stretchers, the peasants from the mountains, and the last pack-mules wind their way between the vast rocky landscape, where the evening rain clouds are gathering, and the hundreds of peasants standing motionless with raised fists. The women are quietly weeping, and the procession seems to be fleeing from the silence of the mountains, with its clatter of hooves amid the melancholy cries of the birds of prey and this surreptitious sobbing.

A fascist flotilla is shelling the port of Valencia, six kilometers away. A fine rain is falling over the city and dripping gently off the orange trees. The workers' syndicates have organized a parade for the children's fête. The children's delegations have demanded film cartoon figures, and the syndicates have constructed enormous cardboard effigies of Mickey Mouse, Felix the Cat, and Donald Duck (preceded nevertheless by a Don Quixote and a Sancho Panza). Of the thousands of children who have come from all over the province for the fête, which is in aid of the refugee children from Madrid, many are without shelter for the night. Along the outer boulevard, the floats, their triumphal procession at an end, now lie abandoned; over a stretch of two kilometers my headlights reveal the talking animals of Disneyland, of a world in which all who are killed come back to life; children with nowhere else to go for the night have settled down beneath the huge cardboard figures, between the legs of the mice and the cats. The enemy flotilla goes on shelling the port, and the animals, shaken by the explosions, nod their heads in the rain above the sleeping children, under the watchful eye of Don Quixote.

These memories of *Man's Hope* remind me that in Spain, in Alsace, in the prison camp, the doctors tended casualties who did not awaken.

In the camp in 1940, a woman walks past the barbed wire fence to which hungry prisoners are clinging. She passes four or five clusters of men, not daring to take the bread out of her bag. A little farther on, the faces will be no less hungry-looking.

At last—from weariness, anxiety, fear of the sentry's return—with an effort she goes up to the wire and takes out of her bag a circular loaf which glitters in the sun:

"Share it, share it!" she hurriedly entreats them.

So many hands shoot out, and no doubt with such an expression on the faces, that she draws back, and the loaf falls outside the wire. In the concerted growl of the prisoners not a word can be heard. She picks up the bread, throws it in, and hurries off without looking at the men, who, smeared with blood from the barbed wire, get to their feet and themselves hurry off, each with a scrap of bread in his hands.

She will be back. It is always the same ones who come.

During the Occupation: one of Colonel Rémy's under-cover escorts. He has to cross a river with a woman on his back and her child in his arms. She is so afraid the child may cry that she gags him, hands him over to the man, and clings round the man's neck; and the escort sets out once more into the night.

An old woman whose name I have forgotten, although I recommended her for a medal after the Liberation. The German tanks are advancing toward a fork in the road, and the woman knows that the right fork leads to the maquis. She walks toward them with a basket on her arm. They question her, and we see her gesticulating and pointing left. The tanks set off in that direction, which will enable us to attack them from the flank. She knows this, and she also knows that they may well come back.

I have also experienced the mockery of fraternity.
"Hail, King of the Jews!"

It begins in a black-market restaurant in Paris in 1943. Five Resistance executives. Lunch dispatched, we are about to slip away. Raguse, the leader of the Gaullist mission in Paris, is being pestered by one of our colleagues, of whom I know nothing except that he is a regular colonel.

"Lancelot," Raguse says to him, "would you mind discussing this little matter with Berger? He knows more about it than I do."

And to me in an undertone:

"For God's sake rescue me from this lunatic. I've got quite enough to think about today."

The others go off with him while the colonel waits for me, and says as soon as I sit down again:

"The point is this. There's a gulf between the army and the intellectuals which seems to be unbridgeable. It isn't. I assure you, my dear fellow, that we have plenty of poets in the army. After the Liberation we must start up a poetry review devoted to army poets. To begin with we'd only print sonnets. Because..."

Flabbergasted, I look at my watch. It's going to go on for some time, and I have an appointment with my courier, Violette, "the best female shot in the British Army," in the garden of the Trocadéro. I must not discourage this fellow resister, who has other qualities besides collecting sonnets; nor must I miss Violette. How infuriating of Raguse! A discussion about sonnets. Promises. What will the Resistance not have promised? Watch, sonnets, review; sonnets, review, watch. Finished at last. Between the door of the restaurant and the entrance to the Métro, I ruminate about what Raguse has said to me on the subject of torture: how many members of the Resistance have been arrested, and therefore tortured, because they spent too long saying good-bye to their cats! And now we are fighting in the very doorway of hell.

Ah, well ... let's go and get Ballataire's documents, which Violette is bringing.

Twenty minutes late—a lot. From the bottom of the Trocadéro steps, I see Violette at the right-hand door. I do not know Ballataire. Is he the little fellow in a beret who is walking toward her? A whistle. Men rush out of the bushes and fling her into a German military vehicle. Ballataire follows them without quickening his step. Has he betrayed her? I walk away toward the Seine with a nonchalant air, hearing my breath panting like the staccato chug of a receding outboard. What if I had arrived on time?

A child goes by rolling a hoop.

I was expecting my new contacts from Violette. Raguse has vanished, and I am leaving tomorrow. My last possible contact in Paris is Camaret, the national leader and hero of the Groupes Francs, the assault units of the Resistance. He was captured after having attacked an Abwehr van in the Boulevard Saint-Michel, two hundred yards from the Préfecture, and freed two of our men. He was tortured, but escaped. Raguse had given me the address of his new hideout. Worth a try. What sort of state will I find him in?

If I find him.

And not before seven o'clock.

I wait for nightfall.

A luxury housing-authority building, so to speak, in the XVth arrondissement. Empty staircase. Second floor, on the left. I knock in accordance with the prearranged signal. Camaret opens. Tall, slim, handsome, a blond Aryan! (in fact he is Jewish) unchanged except for a smile that does not leave his face and that resembles a scar. He examines me beneath the hall light, and nods his bandaged head as though to indicate that he recognizes me. I ask him:

"Are you alone?"

"Yes."

We go into a conventional sitting room with an upright piano, and sit down on a little divan covered in red satin.

"Violette has been arrested," I tell him. "I must find some other contacts."

Violette may (one never knows) have left some notes in her handbag—and people may talk under torture. I know that Camaret has just been tortured. His head is bandaged, and underneath his open shirt dressings are visible.... Torture obsesses me, as it obsesses us all.

"How was she taken?" he asks.

"Betrayed. By a miraculous chance I was late."

I tell him the story.

"Where is she?"

"At the Gestapo headquarters in the Avenue Foch, I suppose. We'll know tomorrow."

"We can't do anything about the Avenue Foch. If they transfer her to the Conciergerie we can have a try. In the meantime, if they know who she is, and they *must* know, things won't be too good. Let's try."

"Your Groupes Francs succeeded once. They won't bring it off again."

He gets up and paces around the little room.

"We could attack the German cars (this time, as you say, there'll be several) in the Avenue Foch itself, before they get to the Étoile.... I say, do you know anything about haute couture?"

"No. I've thought a bit about fashion; it isn't quite the same thing, but..."

"What have you thought about?"

"It would be interesting to know why men wear beards for centuries, and then decide to shave, whereas women change fashions every year.... But what about my contacts?"

"What? Ah, yes."

The radio from London, turned low, begins to broadcast "personal messages."

He starts pacing again, then stops beside a table and scribbles something on a pad.

"This is the military delegate for Paris. He's my London contact now. Have you made a note of it?"

He means: learned it by heart. No one makes a note of anything in the Resistance. I take out my lighter; I crush the slip of charred paper in an ashtray.

"I also need a less senior contact: a radio operator, a courier, another Violette."

"Here's mine. Very badly dressed. Why do women change their wardrobe every year? And why are they so much at the mercy of fashion?"

No sooner has he asked the question than he holds his head between his hands: his face is a mask of pain.

On the radio, General de Gaulle is speaking.

"The answer to the first question seems perfectly simple," I say. "To wear the latest thing before anyone else was to be a fashionable woman, no? But why should it matter to you?"

He sits down and taps his fingers furiously on the table.

"I am in love with an artist. A fashion artist. She designs new models. Charming. A Czech aristocrat. Knowing why one model will work and another not is just as important as knowing how to contact the Paris military delegate, isn't it?"

He resumes pacing, the contorted smile once more on his lips. So contorted that it seems not to belong to him: his superb Siegfried-like looks evoke his former smile, and this grin seems out of place.

"You know, Berger, the Resistance should start up its own fashions. Invisible, of course. Invisible. But we'd recognize them. The radio from London would describe the models. Our female comrades would dress themselves accordingly, at home. Nuns wear their uniform in the convent. Next year's fashions will be based on my friend's designs. I've told her so. When I was interrogated by the Gestapo on the second day all the gray mice were wearing them. In my honor."

He is not joking. Suddenly I begin to understand. I shall not ask him how they tortured him on the first day. After the sonnet-fancying colonel, it seems to be a day for crackpots. Camaret is becoming more and more a changed man—his fixed grin is now playing havoc with his features—but no doubt the contacts he has given me are genuine.

"Well, then, have you any thoughts on the development of fashion, yes or no?"

"What I think is pretty banal...."

"You're not Berger!" he yells, foaming at the mouth. "Berger knows what he thinks, but I've caught you out! You're from the Gestapo! Don't try and ..."

He pulls a gun from under his arm. For the last few seconds I have been expecting something of the kind. Madmen seldom look like madmen, and I remembered a woman friend whom I ran into one day in the Rue du Bac who seemed normal, not to say eloquent: "When I changed rooms at the hospital I could see a tree from my window. I hadn't seen a tree for months. A tree..." Touched but in a hurry, I walked on after the nurse who was pushing my little daughter's pram, with the madwoman at my side. At the very moment when she was adding calmly "I came to life again," she opened her bag and took out a razor blade.

With a blow violent enough to break Camaret's arm, I send the revolver flying and run to the door, my heart beating as violently as when I left the Trocadéro.

Is the Gestapo watching the house? Fingering the trigger of my own revolver, I slip into the blacked-out street. No passerby, no police. Suddenly I stumble and lean against the wall. Opposite me, on the façade of a large building with closed shutters, a huge rectangle of light projected by an open window, like a cinema screen, Camaret's gesticulating shadow, and his shouts echoing through the silence of the listening city:

"Informers, the lot of them! They won't get me! They can go to hell, and those bloody Krauts too! France will lead the world in fashion!"

His yells are punctuated by the radio, turned up to full volume and still broadcasting the "personal messages" from London: "The little fellow has lost his bottle.... The..."

Without slowing down, I watch the shadow of the hero of the Groupes Francs lurching about in the rectangle of light projected onto the façade of the shuttered house across the street. Beneath a sky almost white with the profusion of stars.

The manageress of the hotel at Gramat kneeling in my blood: "It's for the wounded French officer."

The beautiful nun who brought me the Gospel according to St. John and some real coffee. (I was reading an idiotic play in a theater review.) The convent was rather like the Salpêtrière.

Glimpsed through the back window of the German ambulance taking me to prison, the sky streaked with smoke trails from our burning farmhouses, like the trails of the burning oil tanks at the time of the retreat.

In Auvergne, driving along at the foot of the peaks, our gasogene-propelled cars on the way to the Alsatian front like the taxis of the Marne. Brive and Périgueux captured, the maquis groups of Corrèze and Dordogne set off for Alsace with the Alsatians who have liberated their towns with them.

The last letter from Captain Peltre, the first of our men to be killed in the Vosges, to his wife: "I have not forgotten that I have a wife and child, perhaps children, and for your sake as well as my own I dearly value life, value it enough to do my duty—the duty of a man in the fullest sense of the word, who endeavors to give to everyone what it is in him to give of himself, without foolhardiness." Maquisards in forage caps, accustomed to bazookas and the forest, we take up position ahead of the First Armored Division, bogged down in a prehistoric sea of mud. The helmets arrive on the fifth day, and Peltre is killed while distributing them to his men.

We buried him in the cemetery of Froideconche, where all the soldiers whose bodies have been recovered have been buried.

The little girls of the village and the schoolmistress spent the night sewing, and all our graves are decorated with childish flags.

More farmhouses in flames: the battle of Dannemarie. The "volunteer units" attack at dawn. They have all volunteered with the shrug that means it is a matter of course. All night long they have waited, stretched out alongside warm beasts in the rimy fields, while the farmhouses burned on the horizon. Now it is dawn. They attack the German tanks covered in hoarfrost on the right. On the left is the Legion, which does not choose its war. The men who have fought for so long with bare hands, the men who used to steal chickens, advance with the same traditional slow step as the Legionnaires, determined to serve as targets just as imperturbably as the battle-hardened "white caps." Long lines of ambulances return to the field hospital to disgorge their wounded, and messengers bring requests for commando leaders to replace those who have fallen, wave after wave. Already the companies have dispersed for the attack, and nothing can be seen on the left but helmets scattered among the bushes, the fields and the hoarfrost, and white caps on the right. The two waves advance at the same pace. At dawn in the fields of Dannemarie, soaked with the blood of three centuries, the tatterdemalion infantry of the maquis matches the solemn tread of the foremost crack corps of the defunct French Army with a deep reverberation that mingles in my memory with echoes of the imperial guard. All the senior officers having been wounded, the attack will end with me.

How cold it is on earth! The following night, in the light of the moon and the conflagrations, the long procession of German prisoners—like us, four years earlier.

Our weapons captured from the enemy.

Our female stretcher bearers who went out under the shells to pick up the wounded.

Years later, after the return of General de Gaulle, my

"gorilla" friends, ready for the same OAS bomb as me, one
of them engrossed in *Le Canard enchaîné:* Paris...

The adolescent girl in armor who represents Joan of Arc
at the commemorative festivities in Orléans. I told her that
she was the living image of France, and she was to be the
first to write to me when my children died.

The little wire handgrips with which the General kept
himself in training.

At Colombey for his funeral, Ponchardier, the "gorilla"
of the Resistance, the inventor of the word, and the man
who broke open Amiens prison during the Occupation,
now governor of Djibouti, tells me how the Afars and the
Issas set out across the desert as soon as the General's death
was announced to make their signs in the register opened at
Government House. We hurry along beneath the dull gray
sky to the sound of the knell that echoes from all the
churches of France and calls to my mind the bells of the
Liberation. I have already seen the open grave, with the
two enormous wreaths by the side of it: from Mao Tse-
tung and Chou En-lai. At Colombey, in the little church
without a past, there will be the parish, the family, the
Order of the Liberation: a knight's funeral. Here among
the crowd, behind the marines with fixed bayonets, a
peasant woman in a black shawl, like the women of our
maquis in the Corrèze, shrieks: "Why won't they let me
through! He said everybody! He said everybody!" I put my
hand on the shoulder of the nearest marine: "You should
let her through; it would please the General." He swivels

round without a word and without moving a muscle, as though presenting arms to the lowly and the faithful of France—and the woman hobbles toward the church before the roar of the tank which bears the coffin.

At night in the Champs-Élysées down which he once walked, a silent multitude brings to the Arc de Triomphe bunches of rain-soaked marguerites that have not been brought there since the death of Victor Hugo.

It is not that famous walk along the Champs-Élysées that I think of, when France seemed to hear at last the refrain "When you arise from among the dead"; it is the whispering procession of women in the rainy night toward the flag flapping in the wind beneath the echoing Arc of the Étoile. The quivering shafts of the rain dip their lances in the light of the streetlamps standing like ghostly sentinels; an infinite silence broods over Paris; in Peking, the flags are at half-mast above the Forbidden City. Fraternity advances step by step through the night toward the Arc to offer its tribute of flowers, and the Flame, alternately flattened by the wind and springing up again, extinguishes or illumines the streaming faces. Fellowship is often as powerful as death itself.

Plunging, slipping, foundering—springing up again like the Flame at the Arc de Triomphe flattened against the ground by the nocturnal wind. As much as that night in the Champs-Élysées, I am haunted by the Russians and the Germans in the Vistula forest, by the word *convulsive*, and by whirlwinds on the China Sea. But lucidity is returning.

Not only is the examination of my own life repugnant to me, but the propinquity of death makes a mockery of it; not only does death fail to summon up those I have loved, but in this hospital room it drives us out together. Whereas it encourages my memories of fraternity. The striking relationship of fraternity to death remains nonetheless enigmatic. As with madness: Camaret's gesticulating shadow recalls the masked figures carrying the gassed Russians to the Bolgako ambulances.

Ever since *Altenburg*—more than thirty years ago—I have been preoccupied with the thought of fundamental man. Man identical with himself from the earliest civilizations; identical with the townsman of Babylon. Identical with the semi-gorilla who, lifting up his eyes, for the first time felt himself one with the star-studded sky; identical with the walnut trees of Altenburg which were reborn from the dead nuts only a hundred yards from the sculpted saints carved out of the trees of yesteryear. Identical with so many dead—and, in 1943, the Resistance numbered more dead than living. The fraternity of battle creates a profound link between a man and his own people; in the strictest sense of the word, it is a communion.

The sudden revulsion of the soldiers of the Vistula revealed in each one of them the counterpart of the man whom he was meant to fight and whom he was saving—the counterpart of the Spanish mother silently kissing her son's torn body. The Germans of Bolgako, the old peasant woman who sent Hitler's Germans off on the wrong road, were *witnesses*. Of their cause? Almost all of them would have said: "What else could we do?" Nothing more;

human dignity.... Our young dead in the high mountains: "The grandeur of the mountains cannot prevail over a single bloodstain, when it is the blood of one's kin." Our first attack in the Alsatian forest; we could not yet hear the enemy tanks. I looked at the fir trees like cathedral pillars, and at our men being showered with twigs by the machine-gun fire: witnesses—of what?—before the vast indifference of the trees.

Once more the fever returns. As evening approaches with its plaintive murmurings, my jottings begin to dissolve in a warm tide, as though my hands, falling open, were to discover that they were relinquishing life. Confusedly, I...

The attack was less intense than the previous one. I knew that my pen was going to slip from my fingers. Am I, from the House of the Dead, destined to note down only what belongs to life, and from the realm of madness only the lucid moments? We become conscious of our breathing when it is cut off, and of hope when it recedes. The theological virtue called Hope is not to be confused with the insatiable avidity of the gambler as the roulette wheel revolves: it is not the hope of anything. But the fever soon spirits it away. Return through a landscape of dreams.

It sometimes happens that I return to earlier dreams, and recognize them. I am walking through a murky wasteland, strewn with lead pipes and broken tiles and peopled with a multitude of chilly disembodied overcoats wandering between fences stretching endlessly into the distance. A companion, sensing my anguish in spite of my silence, murmurs, vaguely designating this limbo: "It's nothing, sir: it's just the unconscious." In the prisoner-of-war camp in 1940, I gazed at the thousands of shadowy figures in the uneasy light of dawn and thought, It's mankind. Last night, I thought of nothing; I sank into the unknown. I emerge from vast ruins, but I do not remember only ruins. Here is my last dream. The retreat in 1940 filled with dust and roses, peasants setting fire to their hayricks before the arrival of the enemy, while dusk falls in the summer haze. A return to the murky landscape of my previous dream. Then I am surrounded by a solemn darkness. Stars begin to appear. The nascent stars that pervaded Victor Hugo's old age, the constellations of Boaz's dream glittering in the sky of death.

Ecstatic states—outside Christianity, which links them with Christ—are doubtless akin to what overcame me then. But even if hashish, whose religious influence I experienced in Siam, is a powerful intensifier of the music or the divine which we bring to it, it engenders no new thought, offers no discoveries. It would not have told me that these two dreams spoke to me of death. I asked myself no questions. One idea obsessed me: My own death belongs intrinsically to the realm of the unthinkable. *Intrinsically:* the adverb lengthened, deepened, as though intensified by a stimulant, coiled round the professor whose long silhouette with the long nose had filled my memory with its long-limbed movements, and which just then twisted itself into a knot:

"The fascination of the corpse ... The worst purveyor of anxiety ..."

For me, the worst purveyor of anxiety was fainting, the

more so because it was mixed up in my mind with a prolonged coma hovering between life and death. Although fainting is not artificial life, both inhabit the same zone of absence. I had not forgotten: "One thinks: *I* will be *this*"—"this" suggesting catalepsy as much as decomposition.

"My experience of death," the professor had said, "doesn't yet include my own, you know!" My deepest consciousness does not coincide with a particular moment of my past or with my past as a whole, not even in the face of death, since it would have been identical in kind ten years earlier. An inchoate but powerful affirmation of each for himself, which I remembered on entering the hospital, "the incomparable and elusive monster that each man cherishes in his heart." I do not cherish it much anymore, but I am still aware of it. All the more so because if my syncope did not lay bare that inchoate self, it stripped me of the other. To no purpose; stripped nonetheless. I had lost everything, except life. No bearings; scarcely even a body; no identity: *exit*. Consciousness of life is not consciousness of the person. A past existing in the present. The plaints of the Salpêtrière echo those of the prison yard in Shanghai. No longer any images, or almost none; they came crowding in and are now dissolving in swarms, as drug-induced images appear in cycles; my treatment often acts like a stimulant, intensifying confusion and lucidity alternately. One of my characters (which?) hears his recorded voice on a gramophone, and fails to recognize it; the experience, commonplace today, has not lost its symbolic power. We always hear our own voices through our throats, and those of others through our ears. If one were suddenly to hear the voice of another through one's own throat, one would be terrified. I had written that each of us hears the sound of his *life* through his throat, and that of others through his ears, except in fraternity or love. The book was called *La Condition humaine.*

Since then I have had much experience with death. Now, between the threat and the memory, I have found the fundamental consciousness with which Buddhism is familiar. When the ascetic has lost every form of illusion without attaining Enlightenment, he no longer experiences anything but the unfathomable consciousness of existing, the Peace of the Abyss, in the unity of every age of his life. It is less absurd of man to have tried to see himself in God's image than in that of other people, for the reflection offers us only knowledge, whereas consciousness partakes of belief. The mental operation whereby we attempt to imagine ourselves is as distinct from that consciousness as theology is distinct from faith. The humblest person believes in himself because he cannot do otherwise; in a self rather than in nothing—and believes himself nothing rather than believing nothing. The archaic consciousness ascribed to the mind of the human plesiosaur is beyond thought because it is linked to the deepest unconscious, beyond speech. Mute, like the god who can destroy the earth but has nothing to say to man. But present, whatever the living self may be—the self of the ultimate pain that does not want to die; the self of the last victim of *Nacht und Nebel,* or that of the Emperor Andronicus faced with the ultimate torture: "Lord, why do you go on tormenting a broken reed?" An *I am* far beyond the *I think.*

"Since I've been studying butterflies," Méry used to say, "man strikes me as being the only animal that has the misfortune to remember its caterpillar childhood." Hence the emotive power of the corpse, for a man who has died a peaceful death (as almost all do here, the nurses tell me) resembles the living man of yesterday more than the living resemble the children they once were. Does the child evoke its mortal remains?

And if our fundamental consciousness is only the consciousness of being alive, does it not rebel against extinction as the body rebels against strangulation or the men of Bolgako against the asphyxiating gas? The incantation on the Ganges echoes in my mind:

> *. . . unborn, undying,*
> *Never ceasing, never beginning . . .*
> *Worn-out garments are shed by the body:*
> *Worn-out bodies are shed by the dweller*
> *Within the body . . .*

But our saurian brain could only conceive of the eternally dead; they changed lives, joined their Ancestors. Then humanity changed hereafters. . . . The Age of the Enlightenment, which was deist, believed the soul immortal. The planet, heaped with the dead, hears for the first time the thin layer of the living given the name of humanity. Death is a recent and as yet incomplete discovery. The mythical saurian buried within us rejects it as radically as the consciousness of true madmen rejects the world. Fifty millennia of heavens and hells and liberations are crowned with the derisory survival of a dead man's face. "I will be this." The tragedy of agnosticism does not lie in the fact that we regard death as unthinkable, but in the fact that we cannot bring ourselves to do so. At this game, the corpse wins every time. The word *unknowable* insidiously suggests a knowledge that is never attained but that would extend ours; and yet, far from being given to us, the unthinkable must be torn from all the reincarnations and afterlives, from everything that remains, even if only the corpse. The professor is right: man is tied to the corpse by an insectlike embrace that not even fire will loosen, by the mutual gaze of my adolescent couple in the cinema. But my friend had no inkling of the sense in which the corpse is a guarantee of nothingness. Because this nothingness, as against the "nothing" of the unthinkable, is the last form of afterlife. With the ambivalence, the mixture of fear and hope, that attaches to the afterlife—and that my priest in the camp in 1940 attributed to the last hours. Humanity is attached to the corpse as it was once attached to the recumbent effigies of the dead: never has Christendom feared the Last Judgment more than in the age of the Dance of Death.

The Christians of the eleventh century became converted to Christianity in a body when they wrested the famous *robe d'églises* from the Capetian forest; yet they were Christians. I am groping toward the truth so deeply buried within me, as I groped toward the electric light switch in the darkness of my first blackout. The unthinkable is not what is hidden from us. It does not imply that we are impotent; it implies *nothing*.

The unthinkable terrifies humanity, although it alone can deliver humanity. Where is my reverie leading me? Sitting on the running board of a car in the Laut Desert in Persia in the days when it had not yet emerged from the Middle Ages, while the chauffeur is changing a wheel, I talk about religion with Suleiman from Isfahan and his nephew Saidi, the Zionist (the two antiquaries who were to send to the Louvre the fabric supposedly stained with the blood of Alexander the Great). A convoy of lorries, bristling with turbans and hen coops, recedes amid a swarm of flies toward the windmill-studded horizon.

"You know," says the Zionist, "the sura of the Koran which teaches that we cannot understand the world. Jahweh said the same thing to Job long before their prophet! But the mullahs at Shiraz have transformed this story with great excellence. They are quoted everywhere."

He points at the two ruts made in the track by the lorries. A cricket as big as a crayfish has just hopped between them, its antennae raised.

"They say: 'Supposing the lorry had run over the cricket. It wouldn't be quite dead. It would think: I've been run over by a devil. Very big, very strong. You should avoid meeting devils, they kill you.' It might think that this devil is very wicked, but it could not think how an internal combustion engine works. Nor what the engine thinks. Or that it doesn't think anything."

"That's why people must have a Book," says Suleiman,

who was schoolmaster to the Jewish community. "Even the Russians. You told me they had one."

Plump little Suleiman and tall, stooping Saidi remind me of a mustard pot at odds with its spoon, in the eternal solitude.

"Above all you must never bother about other people's engines!" Saidi replies.

For the absolute unknowable is not a realm of doubt, it is as imperious as the successive faiths of humanity, even in this birdless desert, like the desert where Satan appeared to Jesus. The caterpillar must turn into a chrysalis, the chrysalis into a butterfly—and the butterfly not remember either the chrysalis or the caterpillar. Must? The butterfly will never know where the order comes from, in the double sense of the word. But if we are afraid of cancer, we are not afraid of suddenly seeing ourselves grow a third arm. If my poor neighbor had really been possessed by the certainty of knowing nothing about death, he would not have feared it. "Saved," say the religions. Saved at least from dread, lying awake in the darkness, with the spiders' webs hanging in the corners.

"I'm speaking to you as a man who has seen many people die, most of the time very badly," the professor said to me. The dread which I encountered in this room, after my fall and my journey on the little table, had nothing in common with what I *think* about death. Untold numbers of human beings have been terrified since time immemorial by the Beyond, an Apocalyptic beast more rapacious than the scourges of old or the atom bomb because no one escaped it. How could I help and comfort my unfortunate neighbor, if he was doomed? The closer people are to us the blinder we are; but how many Hindus or Buddhists, how many of those who do not know what they believe, would have been delivered from the specter of death by the certainty of not being reborn—Untouchables, foul animals, creatures of despair—and of not being condemned to extinction either? The vocabulary of the East envelops the lunatic metempsychosis of the West, terrified by the hypnotic and absurd "Thou shalt be reborn into nothingness." The professor is right when he talks of transmigration—of that which connects "you will become a corpse" to "you will become a mouse." What weight would this spider-thought have, if the West had not condemned man to his own physical remains? The dread of extinction is as meaningless as the dread of nonbirth, but men believe in extinction as they believe in the devil—they are not aware of it as they are aware of birth. And extinction *requires* the image of the dead. The human mind has lavished countless forms on the beyond, right down to the last immortal soul; extinction being a toss-up, it is the deepest consciousness, that of being alive, that the unconscious subjugates in order to link man to the cadaver. Agnosticism can only speak to death on an equal footing if it too bases itself on faith. Every dialogue with death begins with the irrational. One *knows* that death is unthinkable; no one can be *aware* of it, as my fever, the hospital, the professor have all brought home to me. Agnosticism, when it accepts its own irrationality, when it experiences the unthinkable with the force of faith, discovers in the dread of death the reincarnation of the Dance of Death, both equally impermanent: the closing of the charnel houses has de-materialized that ephemeral dread. . . .

My memory, it has been said, dwells upon my returns to earth, after the cyclone or the tank trap and the events of the Vistula, Spain, and the Resistance—moments that represent epiphanies. The metamorphosis of ignorance of death into awareness of death, the metamorphosis of knowledge into belief—these, surely, belong to the realm of epiphanies? My odyssey outside the earth to bring back the tablets is also an obscure epiphany. The revelation is that nothing can be revealed. The unknown realm of the unthinkable has neither shape nor name.

There is no connection between this evidence and the images of fraternity. A sudden whiff of the scent from the screen of acacias full of the cockchafers of my childhood; the first onset of cold during the Spanish civil war; the first log fire from which I learned the language of memory; the preacher from Los Hurdes on the Madrid front: "An unknown star rose above them. . . ." What epiphanies correspond to the epiphany of the unthinkable? Those of life: precisely when the plane, having survived the cyclone, had landed me in the little terrestrial town with its laundries, its cats in shop windows, and the enormous glove-maker's sign like the hand of fate. Or the first morning after the tank trap, the old peasant woman reconciled to the cosmos like a stone ("When you're old, there's nothing left but wear and tear"); the barns, the extinguished lights, the clothespins so utterly in harmony with the earth in the miraculous revelation of morning. Or the walnut trees of Alsace rising up in the midst of the ring of young shoots and the dead nuts of winter.... If only, one day, on every radio and television set, in the presence of men ready to listen at last, the ultimate prophet were to yell at Death: "There is no extinction!" Humanity does not remember the earthquakes of its religions. St. Paul, St. Francis, Luther, mere episodes. The revolution of Buddhism, a mere vicissitude—the sacred words themselves condemned men to the Wheel, and adepts revealed that the Buddha Amida would finally deliver, in his Pure Land, the myriads of believers who had invoked it by showing compassion to their fellow beings. To pass from the hovel of the Untouchables to the paradise of the Pure Land, vanity of vanities. Vanity, those multitudes saved, a hundred times more numerous than the multitudes putrefied by the Black Death. Insignificance, the great discoveries of the soul, the Eastern Christian after the schism, the Western Christian after the Reformation—man faced with his first encounter with the throes of death, the civilization that seeks to exorcise annihilation with the fear of death. Beneath these clouds drifting through oblivion, the peasants burning their hayricks at nightfall cannot prevail over the benediction of the stars: "I feel my dark night light up with faint stars." The inconceivable has no attributes—not even menace: man no more becomes a scorpion than a damned soul, and no more a nonbeing than a scorpion.

Our bodies resist so powerfully that we cannot strangle ourselves. We do not even grow accustomed to the threat of death; yet this terrible journey is becoming less frequent. My memories of the first one are already growing dim. And no one can doubt the language of the body. Three months ago the top joint of my right forefinger was fractured by a car door. A little later, a tiny furrow as neat as if it had been cut with a chisel appeared above the half-moon; it has gradually advanced, and now divides the nail in half. I have never seen with such clarity the imprint of my life on my body. It alters everywhere imperceptibly, but here as visibly as the red alcohol rises in a thermometer. Weary of the rustling voices of death, on awakening I watch life renewing itself on my fingernail.

But for several days I have put off noting this. The Zen scriptures tell us that the tension that precedes Enlightenment provokes laughter. Shortly before losing consciousness, I saw my cat, Furry, and glimpsed through the darkness the smile of the Cheshire cat in *Alice in Wonderland*. At the moment of keeling over (I had actually left the ground) I felt death recede; I was penetrated, possessed, overwhelmed—as by an unknown presence, like Boaz by the immense blessedness that descended from the Chaldean firmament—by an inexplicably consoling *irony*, which momentarily outstared the worn-out face of death.